City of Flint 32 is covered with ice as she arrives at Ludington, Michigan, after a midwinter crossing—Manitowoc Maritime Museum, Manitowoc, Wisconsin

LAKE MICHIGAN'S
Railroad Car Ferries

by Karl Zimmermann

Roger M. Clemons
Box 102
Bartlett, NH 03812

ANDOVER JUNCTION
PUBLICATIONS
P.O. BOX 1160   ANDOVER, NJ 07821

Ludington, August 2, 1979.—KARL ZIMMERMANN

For Jennifer and Emily

ANDOVER
JUNCTION
PUBLICATIONS
P.O. BOX 1160   ANDOVER, NJ 07821

PUBLISHING DIRECTOR: Joyce C. Mooney
PUBLISHER: Stephen A. Esposito
EDITORIAL AND ART DIRECTOR: Mike Schafer
DESIGN AND LAYOUT: Rick Johnson

Main front cover photo: Ann Arbor's *Viking* sails from Frankfort, Michigan, for Wisconsin on a tranquil summer evening in 1975.—ROBERT E. MOHOWSKI **Inset:** With black coal smoke foaming from her stack, the venerable car ferry *Chief Wawatam* receives a load of freight cars from the Detroit & Mackinac.— HOANG CHI COOK **Back cover:** The lure of the water and waves still beckons travelers in the hurried years of the 20th Century as this 1979 view from the *Viking* attests.—JOE MCMILLAN **Opposite:** Chesapeake & Ohio ferry *Pere Marquette 22* at Ludington in August 1955.—W. P. ELLIS PHOTOGRAPH, C&O HISTORICAL SOCIETY COLLECTION

CONTENTS

By Car Ferry Across Lake Michigan

On a dank May evening in 1979, with the sun already set, Ann Arbor's venerable *City of Milwaukee*—a handsome railroad car ferry built for the Grand Trunk back in 1931—came gliding into the little Wisconsin port of Kewaunee. Once past the breakwater and into the cramped basin of the harbor, the *Milwaukee* began the laborious process of turning to back into the slip. As she swung broadside to my view, the last light in the sky showed her classic lines: lofty pilot house, tall, raked masts and funnels, low superstructure.

She looked much like an ocean-going liner or freighter of an earlier era—though more horizontal in expression, since railroad car ferries required a perfectly flat car deck. Against broken clouds hung a smear of smoke, for the *City of Milwaukee* was an oil-fired reciprocating steamer. She was, in fact, a remarkable survivor: in 1979, the last of the traditional, unmodernized boats of 1920's design to remain in cross-Lake Michigan service.

True, the *Milwaukee* was a relative youngster compared to the 1911 *Chief Wawatam*, then still alive plying the Straits of Mackinac where Lake Michigan's waters mingle with Lake Huron's, but the other extant cross-Michigan boats were either far more modern in aesthetic—Chessie System's *City of Midland 41* and sisters *Spartan* and *Badger*—or dieselized rebuilds of older vessels—Ann Arbor's *Viking* and laid-up *Arthur K. Atkinson.*

My family and I were planning to board the

City of Milwaukee for an overnight cross-lake cruise to Frankfort, Michigan, and back, so we hurried to the slip. This vessel, unlike the other Lake Michigan car ferries then in operation, was officially, by Coast Guard certificate, a "freight boat" and thus could carry only twelve passengers. We wanted to be sure of being among that dozen, since these were the twilight years for the significant transport of railroad freight cars on Lake Michigan.

While waiting for the *Milwaukee* to dock at Kewaunee, we read the historical marker that stood near Slip 1 and learned that Lake Michigan carferry service had begun there on Sunday, November 27, 1892, when *Ann Arbor No. 1* departed with 22 cars of flour bound from Minneapolis to England, Scotland, and Ireland. As soon as our vessel was made fast, we strode across the loading apron and, passing under the raised guillotine-like sea gate, walked into the cavernous maw of the car deck. We picked our way among freight cars that were intimidatingly huge in such close quarters, stepping gingerly among the rail clamps always affixed at each end of each cut of cars to secure them, and the chains and jacks used when rough weather required "full gear." We clattered up the long, steep, narrow metal stairs to the spar deck and the passenger accommodations.

The boat had a dozen staterooms, but only five were being used for passengers, with the rest assigned to crew. To be sure of getting a room, I rushed to the purser's window, only to find it closed. The waitress in the dining room

> "Ann Arbor's venerable City of Milwaukee ... came gliding into the little Wisconsin port of Kewaunee."

PROLOGUE PHOTOGRAPHS BY KARL ZIMMERMANN

5

suggested that the purser was probably down on the dock supervising the unloading. Since there turned out to be only one other passenger, and he didn't want a stateroom, I needn't have worried.

"As she swung broadside to my view, the last light in the sky showed her classic lines...."

Before long, an Alco C430 diesel in bright-red Green Bay & Western paint showed up and began unloading freight cars from the boat, to the accompaniment of the groaning and squealing of metal on metal. Though it might seem an easy matter to yank out the two dozen cars from the boat's four tracks and replace them with another two dozen for the return trip, the process was complicated by the need to keep the load balanced. The crew began by emptying the center tracks, then one-half of one outside track, then all of the other, then finally the remainder of the first. Then they reversed the procedure to load. Even with precautions, the boat listed alarmingly. (Back in 1909, an Ann Arbor boat had capsized from careless loading of iron-ore cars.)

Ultimately, well after dark, all freight cars were aboard, and the purser raised his window and sold me two adult and two child tickets—continuous round trips at reduced prices, which included a meal—plus a stateroom both ways, all for $68.50. Then he rummaged around for a key that would fit and, after trying a few, let us into the first cabin on the port side.

We found the *City of Milwaukee*'s interior configuration as deliciously archaic as her exterior lines. Forward was the observation lounge, window-lined and furnished in ancient dark wicker. Behind that was the wood-paneled central saloon—really just a wide hallway with inward-facing chairs and benches—off which the staterooms opened. Aft of the saloon was a small dining room whose skylight-like clerestory, rimmed with light bulbs, spoke of former elegance. Our stateroom, paneled in hardwood, contained two comfortable berths (albeit with modest headroom), a cold-water wash basin, and a screened window with wooden blinds.

Hastily we settled our gear so we could be on deck when the *Milwaukee* maneuvered out of the harbor, then sailed past the lighthouse at the end of the breakwater and into a vast, starless Lake Michigan night. After tucking our daughters into their berth, my wife and I went back out on deck again, where we popped the cork of a split of champagne and, from plastic glasses, toasted our own bon voyage.

Later, alone, I walked lap after lap around the spar deck, reliving childhood memories of transatlantic crossings on ocean liners. The pungent freshness of the air, the friendly glow of the deck lights, the shrill whine of wind in the rigging, the rush and surge of water past the hull, the cozy comfort of any lee nook (but particularly the shed that housed the winch, where leaking steam was warm and fragrant): These pleasures were hard to categorize but worth at least $68.50. When I finally went to bed, an open window allowed the crash of water to be my lullaby, and I was soon asleep.

Sometime later, discordant notes intruded. An amplified rattle resonated through the boat like doomsday, followed by a high-pitched, high-volume screeching. We were docking at Frankfort—or Elberta, technically, across Lake

Betsie from Frankfort. The car ferries, which loaded from the stern and thus had to back into their slips, routinely dropped anchor for added maneuverability when berthing, and the *Milwaukee* also used cables to winch herself in. Shortly after I identified these sounds they ceased and I dozed off again, undisturbed by the switching of freight cars.

The next time I awoke it was gray morning outside our window, so we were up quickly and into the dining room for breakfast. This small, workaday room, though it had more in common with a friendly local diner than the dining room aboard the *Queen Mary*, served hearty meals. We ordered from the the breakfast offerings listed on the blackboard: "Malto meal, sausage-eggs, hot cakes, hash browns." Midday dinner and evening supper ran along the same lines—tasty, plentiful, plain. There was a long table with checkered cloth for crew and three smaller ones with white linen for passengers. In the dining room as elsewhere aboard, we had the sense of being slightly unexpected yet welcome guests aboard a working freight boat.

By the time we had finished breakfast and walked on deck, Wisconsin was in sight, and by midmorning we were back on dry land in Kewaunee.

Sadly, this particular voyage can no longer be made; the *City of Milwaukee* was retired in 1982 when all Ann Arbor carferry service ended, though she is currently moored awaiting restoration as a museum ship at her final home port of Elberta. *Chief Wawatam* steamed to her demise in 1984, though the truncated hull of this lost maritime treasure survives as a barge at Sault Ste. Marie.

The happy news involves the former Chesapeake & Ohio's *Badger*, which was returned to steam in 1992, plying between Ludington, Michigan, and Manitowoc, Wisconsin, under the auspices of the newly formed Lake Michigan Carferry Service, but carrying only automobiles and passengers and operating only in summer. A successful inaugural season assured that the great tradition of Lake Michigan car ferries would live on for at least a while longer.

In the chapters that follow, those vessels that sailed into the twilight on Lake Michigan's waters are remembered and chronicled, along with their predecessors.

"As soon as the vessel made fast, we strode across the loading apron...."

"Before long an Alco C430 in bright-red Green Bay & Western paint showed up and began unloading freight cars from the boat...."

"Aft of the saloon was a small dining room whose skylight-like clerestory, rimed with light bulbs, spoke of former elegance...."

7

 # 1 *Chessie's Fleet*

On the boat deck of the *Spartan*, one of Chesapeake & Ohio Railway's final trio of Lake Michigan car ferries, two seamen sitting on a bench marked "crew only" were busy at their handicraft. As the *Spartan* beat her way at a brisk eighteen miles per hour from Milwaukee across the lake to her home port of Ludington, Michigan, these men were off watch and enjoying a calm, sunny August afternoon.

Dexterously using shears and pliers, from discarded beer cans they shaped delicate, filagreed miniature rocking chairs that they'd offer for sale to passengers. Here was the modern version of the ancient seamen's custom of filling off-duty time with crafts: comtemporary scrimshaw, using materials found at hand. (Empty beer cans were certainly as plentiful aboard the *Spartan* as whalebone had been on Captain Ahab's *Pequod*.)

Such maritime traditions exerted a strong influence on the personalities of the C&O boats—and on all the railroad car ferries, for that matter. But there was a genuine duality in their make-up, since their railroading ties were strong as well. After all, their primary function had been to tote freight cars (though eventually automobiles would become more important

Opposite: The *Spartan* (left) and *Badger* (right) are brand new in this publicity photo; the boats' names appear in small lettering on their black hulls, an early practice. These vessels were the first (and only) car ferries to have welded hulls; because the technology was new and uncertain, traditional riveted construction was used below the car deck.— C&O RAILWAY PHOTOGRAPH, C&O HISTORICAL SOCIETY COLLECTION **Above:** On a May morning in 1979, the *Spartan* sails out of the dawn and into Manitowoc.—KARL ZIMMERMANN **Right:** The *Badger* enters the harbor at Kewaunee, sailing past the old Lifesaving Service station on a bright and still morning in the spring of 1981.— TOM POST **Below:** Perched on the deck of the *City of Midland 41* arriving Ludington on a frigid February afternoon in 1971, the photographer recorded *Pere Marquette 21* and the *Badger* in port.—MIKE SCHAFER

Above and right: The car deck of a ferry was an imposing space, particularly at night; it stood in direct contrast to the comfortable rooms for passengers just one deck above. On this night in 1953, a nearly new *Spartan* is loaded and ready to leave Ludington; wheel clamps have been put in place.—BOTH PHOTOS, C&O RAILWAY, C&O HISTORICAL SOCIETY COLLECTION
Below: The *Spartan*'s builder's plate tells a story: of a reciprocating steamer delivered well into the diesel era for a coal-hauling railroad by a shipbuilder new to car ferries.—KARL ZIMMERMANN

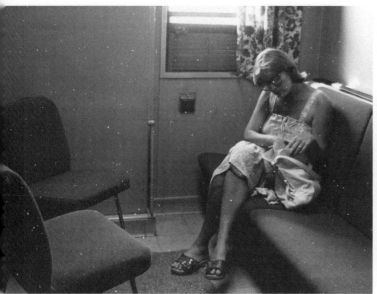

Aboard the *Spartan* in August 1979, both cabins and dining room are evocative of railroading's streamline era.—KARL ZIMMERMANN

cargo), and they were run by railroads.

The *Spartan*'s railroad heritage was suggested in many ways beyond the once-familiar Chessie System "sleeping cat" logo carried in the 1970's and early 1980's on the boat's broad, tapering funnel, where it looked even more graceful than on the angular nose of a diesel locomotive. On the boat deck aft, beyond where the sailors were transforming beer cans into art, the dining room was like a wide dining car with lake views. The spar deck, just below, was dominated by a huge lounge accommodating as many as 200 passengers; here and elsewhere the finish and hardware were evocative of passenger cars in the streamline era. There were also 44 outside and 16 inside staterooms on the spar deck; noting beds that fold out of walls and sofas that make into berths, the seasoned rail traveler felt right at home—and recognized the fabrics and pastel wall colors as typical of Pullman cars built in the early 1950's, when the *Spartan* was launched.

On the next deck down, the car deck, four tracks held two dozen freight cars—give or take a few, depending on what type they were. In the bowels of the ship, automatic stokers fed Chessie-hauled coal into fireboxes heating the water-tube boilers that provided steam for the twin Skinner Unaflow engines. The *Spartan* and the *Badger*, her identical sister, entered service in 1952—the last coal-fired steamers of substantial size ever built in the United States, a distinction they owe to the Chesapeake & Ohio Railway's marriage to coal.

The C&O—or its predecessor in the carferry business, the Pere Marquette Railway—was the largest operator of railroad ferries on Lake Michigan. Actually, the heritage of Chessie's boats goes back even beyond the Pere Marquette's formation in 1900, since two of the line's three predecessors had been operating car

ferries since 1897: the Flint & Pere Marquette from Ludington to Manitowoc, Wisconsin, and the Detroit, Grand Rapids & Western from Muskegon, Michigan, to Milwaukee.

The Flint & Pere Marquette Railway had been chartered in Michigan in 1857 to haul logs from Saginaw to mills at Flint—and, eventually, to reach Lake Michigan at the port of Pere Marquette, across the river from the burial place of Father Jacques Marquette, the Jesuit missionary and explorer. The railroad didn't get there until 1874, by which time its namesake town was being called Ludington, after a Chicago lumberman. Connecting cross-lake service began in 1875 with the *John Sherman*, a chartered side-wheeler. Beginning in 1893, the railroad fielded its own fleet of "break-bulk" steamers (boats requiring transloading of commodities); sail-assisted sisters F&PM No. 1 and No. 2 were the first, and No. 3, No. 4, and No. 5 followed between 1887 and 1890.

As forests were lumbered out and F&PM looked to develop its cross-lake traffic, the inefficient rail-boat-rail cargo transfers of the break-bulk steamers stood as an impediment. Wooden-hulled *Ann Arbor No. 1* and *Ann Arbor No. 2* had shown the way by beginning Lake Michigan carferry service in 1892 between Kewaunee and Frankfort; five years later F&PM came along with the *Pere Marquette*—similar but better. In particular, its steel hull provided the ice-breaking capability so essential in the year-round service that car ferries were to provide for nearly a century.

Three hundred and thirty-seven feet long, with a beam of 56 feet, the *Pere Marquette* could carry thirty freight cars on four tracks—statistics that would remain remarkably constant throughout all the years of carferry evolution. (The *Spartan* and *Badger*, the most modern

Above: With departure from Milwaukee imminent, the *Badger*'s captain has snapped on the bow spotlight to help him slip safely out of the harbor.—Tᴏᴍ Pᴏsᴛ **Left:** Dark hardwood paneling gave the small, windowless lounge of the *City of Saginaw* a masculine air in this 1970 view. The vinyl-covered chairs have replaced the wicker chairs seen in the brochure reproduced on page 21.—Mɪᴋᴇ Sᴄʜᴀꜰᴇʀ **Below left:** In March 1970, the *Spartan*'s lounge is welcoming—attractive, if functional in appearance.—Rᴜss Pᴏʀᴛᴇʀ

ferries, measured just 394 by 60, carrying 34 standard 40-foot cars on four tracks.) With her twin stacks and single cabin deck, this trend-setting vessel, designed by Robert Logan, would become the essential prototype for virtually all Lake Michigan car ferries for more than three decades.

As its dowry, Detroit, Grand Rapids & Western had brought to the 1900 PM wedding the wooden *Muskegon*, built in 1895. She became the *Pere Marquette 16*, while the *Pere Marquette* added the suffix *15* (though only unofficially, up until 1924), bringing both boats into the convention of numerical nomenclature begun with the break-bulk steamers, which at the time of the carferry renamings had the designation "Pere Marquette" added to their numbers. (PM also operated

Above: Rails were a lifeline to the ferries. Having exchanged freight cars with the Green Bay & Western at Kewaunee on a July day in 1972, the *Spartan* departs for Ludington.—MIKE SCHAFER **Right:** The buffet in the *City of Midland 41*'s dining room has the feel of the 1940's.—THREE PHOTOS, THIS ROW, JOE MCMILLAN **Below right:** A crewman rakes ashes from the *City of Midland 41*'s firebox.—MIKE SCHAFER

Detroit River car ferries, which were numbered downward from 14.)

Business boomed, and PM quickly introduced an additional quartet of carferry sisters, all built by American Ship Building and all designed by Robert Logan. *Pere Marquette 17* arrived in 1901, *Pere Marquette 18* in 1902, and *Pere Marquette 19* and *20* in 1903. These boats were nearly identical, differing somewhat in powering but primarily in the amount of passenger accommodation (the latter two had none, being intended for unscheduled sailings in response to the fluctuating demands of rail traffic).

In September 1910, *Pere Marquette 18* foundered en route from Ludington to Milwaukee and sank, taking Captain Peter Kilty—last seen atop the "flying bridge," an

unusual feature of some of these earlier vessels—and some 25 crew and passengers down with her. The abruptness of the sinking—while sister *Pere Marquette 17* stood helplessly by—led all the Lake Michigan carferry operators to equip new vessels from that time forward with sea gates, and to retrofit existing vessels. A nearly identical replacement was ordered immediately and, constructed by American Ship Building's South Chicago yard with remarkable alacrity, entered service in January 1911. PM's decision to call this boat *Pere Marquette 18* after her stricken predecessor must have raised some eyebrows at the time; perhaps a passion for numerical completeness and order overcame any superstitious queasiness.

The final evolutionary step in classic Lake Michigan carferry design came with *Pere Marquette 21* and *Pere Marquette 22*, a pair of handsome sisters—similar to the Logan boats, though a bit bigger—delivered in 1924 by Manitowoc Shipbuilding Company. These vessels, designed in-house by the builder, are the quintessential expression of the traditional car ferry. Their design was duplicated four more times—in *Ann Arbor No. 7* and in the *Grand Rapids*, *Madison*, and *City of Milwaukee* for Grand Trunk. Since *No. 7* became the dieselized *Viking*, and since the *City of Milwaukee* steamed, virtually unmodified, through the 1970's and has been preserved, this outstanding aesthetic expression has had a gratifying longevity.

Soon after the three railroads' consolidation into the Pere Marquette (Chicago & West

Carferry evolution: Early members of the fleet were the *Pere Marquette* (1896, built for the Flint & Pere Marquette and later renamed *Pere Marquette 15*; *Pere Marquette 17* (1901); *Pere Marquette 18* (1902); *Pere Marquette 19* (1903); and *Pere Marquette 20* (1903). The latter two were built without passenger accommodations, which accounts for the amidships gap in the superstructure, with the funnels springing right from the spar deck.—ALL PHOTOS THIS PAGE, C&O RAILWAY, C&O HISTORICAL SOCIETY COLLECTION

Michigan was the one of the trio without car ferries) had been completed in 1900, ex-DGR&W Milwaukee service was moved from Muskegon to Ludington. With the addition of Kewaunee as the third, most northerly Wisconsin port in 1903, the three-fingered hand reaching west across Lake Michigan from Ludington had taken a form that was destined to last nearly eight decades.

The C&O slips on Pere Marquette Lake at Ludington were still an impressive summer place to watch boats as the 1980's dawned, though 1979 was the last full year of service to all three Wisconsin ports. On occasion the entire extant fleet— the *City of Midland 41*, as well as the *Spartan* and *Badger*— were there under steam, filling the air with coal smoke. The ticket office was a long, low building of gray clapboard that said C&O, whether deep in the hills of West Virginia at Quinnimont or Thurmond or on the shores of Lake Michigan at Ludington.

At slips Nos. 2 and 3, spidery wooden trestles hoisted curved automobile ramps up to boat-deck level, where the *City of Midland 41* could accommodate 50 automobiles, and the *Spartan* or the *Badger* 17. (Similar ramps had been built

Pere Marquette Carferry 19

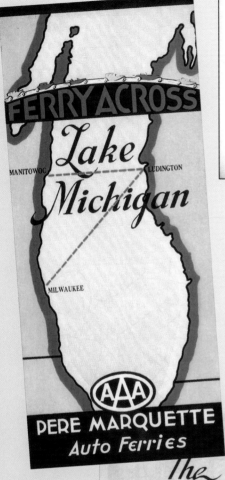

FERRY ACROSS Lake Michigan

MANITOWOC — LUDINGTON

MILWAUKEE

AAA

PERE MARQUETTE *Auto Ferries*

Left and below: *Pere Marquette 21* adorns a PM/American Automobile Association brochure dating from the 1930's.— C&O Railway, C&O Historical Society collection **Above:** Carferry postcards—such as this one of *Pere Marquette 19*—were very common through the years, providing excellent free advertising for the various companies.—Art Chavez collection **Above right:** Ticket stock issued under the affiliated C&O/B&O system.—Karl Zimmermann collection

LAKE MICHIGAN **Autoferry Service**

CHESAPEAKE AND OHIO RAILWAY

B 51512

PERE MARQUETTE *Auto Ferries*

The **SHORT CUT** *for* **MOTORISTS** *in and out of* **MICHIGAN and WISCONSIN**

COMMODIOUS STATEROOMS - EXCELLENT MEALS -

LOW COST

Between Michigan and Wisconsin, nearly a day's drive may now be saved by taking the Pere Marquette Ferry across Lake Michigan. This route avoids the long detour around the base of Lake Michigan, and permits direct-line travel between the beautiful vacation regions of the States of Michigan and Wisconsin.

Not only are driving time and mileage saved, but a delightful break in the motor trip is thus afforded at low cost. The nine great steel steamers in the Pere Marquette fleet are the largest and finest car ferries on the Great Lakes. In addition to ample storage facilities for automobiles, motorcycles, motor trucks and trailers, each of these modern ships provides outside sleeping staterooms, a comfortable lounge and a large dining room for passengers.

For reservations and complete information call or address the nearest representative shown in the list on the back page.

SCHEDULE OF RATES

	MANITOWOC LUDINGTON FERRY (in either direction)	MILWAUKEE LUDINGTON FERRY (in either direction)
PASSENGERS:		
One fare	$2.50	$3.00
Round Trip	4.00	5.50
Berth	1.50	2.00
Stateroom	3.00	4.00
PASSENGER CARS:		
115-inch wheelbase and under	$4.95	$5.50
116-inch to 122-inch wheelbase	6.05	6.60
123-inch to 129-inch wheelbase	7.15	7.70
130-inch wheelbase and over	8.25	8.80
TRUCKS OR BUSES:		
105-inch wheelbase and under	$ 8.80	
106-inch to 114-inch wheelbase	12.10	
114-inch wheelbase and over	.99 per foot over-all measurement	
TRAILERS—MOTORCYCLES:		
Two-wheel or truck trailer	5.50 extra	
Four-wheel trailer	7.70 extra	
Motorcycle	3.30	
Motorcycle with sidecar	4.40	

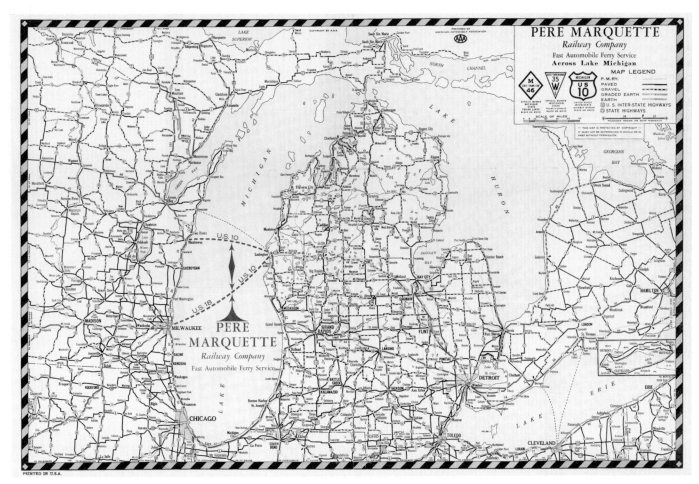

at Milwaukee and Manitowoc, but not at Kewaunee, where autos could be handled only on the car deck.) Crew members loaded and unloaded vehicles, riding to or from the cars by hanging onto an ingenious vertical conveyor belt of an elevator, with foot and hand holds. In earlier years they had donned clean white driving jackets when loading or unloading automobiles.

The last surviving C&O trio fell modern on the eye, daughters of the streamlined aesthetic— as much as an essentially foresquare car ferry can be, since its car deck must be level, prohibiting the sheer that traditionally lent grace to ships. The need to allow the four railroad tracks to run parallel for as much of the boat's length as possible also mandated this boxiness. But through rounded edges here and there, the sharp outward tapering of the bow, and the broad stripe of white that marked the spar deck against the otherwise black hull, the boats made a modern visual statement. The single conical funnel was perhaps the one detail that best expressed the design intent. And this modernism went beyond aesthetics, for C&O's trio were well suited to the realities of traffic balance in the last great days of the Lake Michigan car ferries.

For these ferries, the modern era may be said to have begun in 1929, when the C&O (which just recently had absorbed the Pere Marquette,

though the smaller road would maintain its separate identity until 1947) introduced the *City of Saginaw 31* and the *City of Flint 32*. These boats were pioneers and trend-setters in many ways, including a greatly intensified concern for the handling of passengers, who were coming to the boats in much increased numbers as tourism burgeoned. The inclusion aboard of 43 comfortable staterooms attested to that concern, as did the general upgrading of passenger facilities. Up to this time, passengers had been decidedly secondary.

The *City of Saginaw 31* and *City of Flint 32* were the first Pere Marquette boats to carry names, though the tradition of numbering was simultaneously retained. These boats were mechanical innovators, too: They were turbo-electric powered and had automatic stokers. The boats were relative speedsters, capable of eighteen miles per hour; fourteen had been the previous standard. As a new page in carferry history, these twins were were given numbers in a new decade.

Then, with the *City of Midland 41*'s maiden voyage on March 12, 1941, the final steps were taken in catering to passenger comfort. She was the first car ferry with two decks for passengers; she offered 72 staterooms, including a dozen "master rooms"—parlors with private showers.

For years, the Pere Marquette/American Automobile Association brochures featured maps of Middle America, touting the ferries as a shortcut for motorists heading for upper Midwest vacationlands. The Ludington-Manitowoc crossing was actually part of U.S. Route 10.—C&O RAILWAY, C&O HISTORICAL SOCIETY COLLECTION

17

Perhaps the most beautiful car ferries ever designed were the six sisters delivered by Manitowoc Shipbuilding Company to Pere Marquette, Ann Arbor, and Grand Trunk between 1924 and 1931. *Pere Marquette 21*, shown here at Manitowoc, the port of her birth, was the first.—C&O Railway, C&O Historical Society collection

Provision was made on the boat deck for carriage of fifty automobiles, though—because of war-mandated gasoline restrictions and the resultant constriction of automobile travel—it would be years before the ramps were constructed at the slips to allow this space to be used. At 389 feet and 3,968 tons, the *City of Midland 41* was then the largest car ferry on the lakes.

Because the turbo-electric powering of the *City of Saginaw 31* and *City of Flint 32* had fallen into disfavor in the decade-plus since their launching, the *City of Midland 41* was equipped with a pair of Skinner Unaflow reciprocating steam engines. With quick reversing characteristics, they are particularly well suited to Great Lakes carferry operations, where boats must routinely dock stern-first, without tugs, and jockey back and forth to break ice in winter. This was as marked an innovation in powering as the *City of Saginaw 31* and *City of Flint 32*'s turbo-electrics had been; therefore, another new decade of numbering was begun with *City of Midland 41*.

The machine-age, metallic, streamlined aesthetic of the *City of Midland 41* was typical of 1939, the year the ship was ordered. Essentially the same styling was retained for the *Badger* and *Spartan*, ordered a dozen years later. They were built by Christy Corporation of Sturgeon Bay, Wisconsin, while all the C&O's other "modern" boats—Nos. 21, 22, 31, 32 and 41—were products of Manitowoc Shipbuilding Company. Perhaps somewhat quixotically, and due to C&O's loyalty to the coal it hauled, they too were powered by Skinner Unaflow engines, though some voices had spoken strongly in favor of diesels. The *Midland*, *Spartan*, and *Badger* all met the eighteen-miles-per-hour speed standard set by *City of Saginaw 31* and *City of Flint 32*. The three newest boats each were built to handle 34 freight cars; by the time the vessels ended

their railroad careers, however, the growth in size of freight cars had made 24 a more realistic estimate.

The *Spartan* and *Badger* were christened together on September 6, 1952, honoring Michigan State University and the University of Wisconsin respectively in being named for their mascots. In a break with tradition, no numbers were officially assigned to these boats, though the *Spartan* was routinely referred to as 42 and the *Badger* as 43. These numbers appeared in lieu of names on the arrivals and departure board in the Ludington ticket office, on official C&O memoranda, and on the ships' linen and equipment.

In 1953, also as part of the $20 million expansion program that provided the *Spartan* and *Badger*, came the modernization of *Pere Marquette 21* and *Pere Marquette 22*. They were lengthened by forty feet; received Skinner Unaflow engines, which enabled them to achieve the eighteen-miles-per-hour standard; and were crowned with the single tapered funnel—the mark of modernism—which *31* and *32* had worn since 1942 and the *Midland*, *Badger* and *Spartan* always. Passenger accommodations aboard *21* and *22* had already been enlarged, back in 1937, to offer forty cabins instead of a dozen as built.

This concluded the era of expansion for the C&O car ferries, though they were to hold their own through the 1950's and 1960's—to the point where the railroad did give serious thought to adding a third sister to the *Badger/Spartan* duo. This immediate post-modernization period would prove the zenith for the C&O fleet; during one year, the boats made 6,986 crossings, carrying some 205,000 passengers, 71,000 automobiles and 204,460 freight cars. In 1955, the automobile ramps were finally erected at the Chicago & North Western slip in Manitowoc and the No. 2 slip at Ludington, enabling the three newest

ferries to load automobiles on their boat decks. In 1960, ramps were added at the No. 3 slip at Ludington and at Jones Island in Milwaukee.

"The finest ships of their types in the world," according to a C&O brochure of that era, "Chessie's fleet of seven fast vessels operate round the clock every day throughout the year." Specifically, there were three daily round trips to Milwaukee (four in summer), a crossing that from Ludington took six hours. Service from Ludington to Manitowoc was twice-daily and to Kewaunee once; crossing time in each case was four hours.

In 1963, C&O took control of the Baltimore & Ohio Railroad, beginning a period of coordinated operations as "The C&O/B&O Railroads." In the long run, this affiliation would have a devastating effect on the ferries, since B&O's Chicago operations would provide an increasingly attractive all-rail alternative to the ferries. But in the short run it was a blessing, since it brought B&O's aggressive passenger department—under the leadership of Paul Reistrup, later president of Amtrak—into the picture.

Freight traffic—characterized by westbound

Above: In September of 1943, *Pere Marquette 22* leaves slip No. 3 at Ludington; *Pere Marquette 18* is tied up to the left.—C&O RAILWAY, C&O HISTORICAL SOCIETY COLLECTION **Below:** Though Lake Michigan car ferries were renowned for their ice-breaking ability, they did occasionally get frozen in—as was the case with *Pere Marquette 22.*—KARL ZIMMERMANN COLLECTION

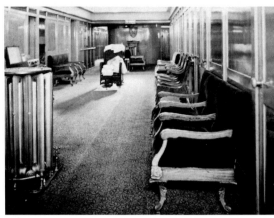

Left: As built in 1939, the *City of Saginaw 31* had a single tall stack.—C&O Railway, C&O Historical Society collection **Above:** Traditional carferry design featured a center saloon with inward-facing lounge chairs and circular radiators to keep the area cozy.—Rose Hawley Museum, Ludington, Michigan

paper products, auto parts, chemicals, and salt and eastbound beer, wood pulp, lumber, and heavy equipment—peaked in 1959; though it held up well through the 1960's, it was becoming increasingly clear that whatever future the boats might have was linked to automobiles and passengers. Accordingly, B&O's passenger traffic managers got busy refining the product, then marketing it. They created attractive "Chessie Cruise" packages: bargain round trips, available from Ludington, Manitowoc, or Milwaukee, that included two meals. Overnight schedules were modified for more convenient departure and arrival times and, following a time-honored tradition aboard Pullman sleeping-cars, offered early boarding and delayed disembarkation. Snack bars, cocktail lounges, televisions and

additional deck chairs were added aboard the three newest boats.

A clever and aggressive advertising campaign, built largely around the monicker "The Good Ferry," was carried forward in magazines and newspapers. Headlines included "The Great American Ferry Tale," "Chessie the Good Ferry," "The Good Ferry is Alive and Well—(Somewhere Between Wisconsin and Michigan)," "The Good Ferry is Really a Double Crosser," and "Take a Lake Break." There was even an ad in *Playboy* Magazine in 1968 promoting "The $9.95 Ocean Cruise, Sort Of."

But by the early 1970's, with the C&O/B&O passenger department history due to the creation of Amtrak, a malaise was beginning to set in. Briefly put, the C&O had lost interest in operating the boats and wanted nothing more than to be rid of them as expeditiously as possible—booming passenger business or not. Though the consequences of that wish were complex, the reasons for it were simple. The coal-fired, steam-powered boats were hopelessly labor-intensive and expensive to fuel, and the technology of railroading had changed sufficiently to render them obsolete in their original function: hauling freight cars.

When trains were short and the Chicago-area yards congested enough to cause multiple-day delays, the C&O ferries were an admirable short cut, allowing much prompter, more reliable delivery of cars. But by the 1970's railroads, questing for greater productivity, routinely ran trains of well over a hundred cars; in addition, unit trains, "run-through" operations, and pre-blocking greatly reduced delays in Chicago, to the point where C&O claimed it could move cars

By the time the *City of Saginaw 31* and *City of Flint 32*—seen on these billboards—were conceived, motorists made up a market worth attracting, so the railroad posted advertisements on both sides of the lake, offering enticement or directions. **Above left:** This billboard on the Michigan side was erected in 1938, before the vessel it pictured was launched. **Above right:** This more homespun one was posted near Bellevue, Wisconsin, with directions to Kewaunee. "The sign was constructed by Mr. Kent in his shop at Ludington," reported Mr. F. A. Young, general passenger agent, in his letter of August 21, 1939, to Mr. Walter S. Jackson, advertising manager, "and I believe you will agree that he did a first class job."—C&O Historical Society collection

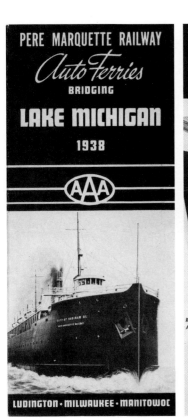

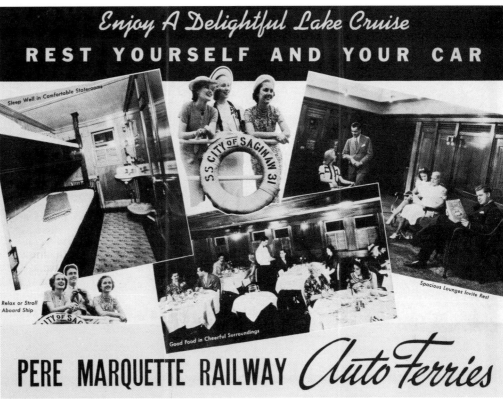

Above and above right: For decades the Pere Marquette and the American Automobile Association jointly issued folders for the ferries. This brochure dating from 1938 features the *City of Saginaw* rushing through waves that had been painted by an artist. The *City*'s staterooms, dining room and lounge were illustrated inside.—C&O Historical Society collection

Below left: At Ludington, C&O box cars are pushed onto the *City of Flint 32*'s car deck. **Below:** Automobiles were carried there too, as shown in this July 1947 view at Milwaukee. Attendants dressed in white smocks parked cars and then returned them to customers at the end of the voyage.—Both photos, C&O Railway, C&O Historical Society collection

The *City of Midland 41* ushered in a completely new aesthetic for Pere Marquette (soon to be C&O) boats, with her streamlined exterior and stylishly modern interior spaces, such as the lounge and dining room.—BOTH PHOTOS, C&O RAILWAY, C&O HISTORICAL SOCIETY COLLECTION

Captain Arthur J. Altschwager aboard the *City of Midland 41* in September 1946. —C&O RAILWAY, C&O HISTORICAL SOCIETY COLLECTION

around Lake Michigan more quickly than across it. In any event, one unarguable conclusion was that the full crew size of five (since reduced even further) to operate a 125-car train compared very favorably with the carferry crew complement of 68 in summer (with many passengers to serve) or 55 in winter to move perhaps 24 freight cars per trip across the lake. Fuel costs on the boats were astronomical, too, with each using 70 tons of coal a day on average. In both fuel and personnel, coal-fired steamers were expensive.

C&O responded to these changed conditions with a memo dated September 12, 1971, on "Controlled Withdrawal of Great Lakes Traffic," instructing salespeople to promote alternatives to the ferries. "Station Agents," the memo said in part, "should be instructed not to insert the C&O cross-lake route on waybills where they have the power to choose the route . . . ." These tactics proved successful, and freight carloadings dropped from 77,387 in 1970 to 29,092 in 1975 and 26,987 in 1976. (They had been approximately 132,000 in 1961.) Passenger patronage, however, remained stable.

Part of the "Controlled Withdrawal" plan— also called the "Chicago Plan," for the replacement all-rail route around the lake to the south—had been to shrink the fleet; by the end of 1972 the *City of Flint 32* (out of service since 1967) had been sold to Norfolk & Western for conversion to a barge, the *City of Saginaw 31* had burned at Manitowoc (almost incinerating the *Chief Wawatam*, which was there for repairs), and *Pere Marquette 21* and *Pere Marquette 22* had been retired. Then on March 18, 1975, the C&O filed with the Interstate Commerce Commission to abandon all its routes, claiming losses of up to $4 million a year. (In 1972, a more

limited request, to discontinue just the Kewaunee route, while Ann Arbor discontinued its service to Manitowoc, had been denied.)

After years of deliberation, the ICC in 1978 gave qualified approval under a compromise agreement sometimes known as the "Kewaunee Package", which would have allowed termination of service to Milwaukee immediately, to Manitowoc in 1980, and to Kewaunee in 1983. The C&O in return agreed to hold the rate structure constant, thus temporarily protecting the very vulnerable Green Bay & Western. (The 250-mile Winona, Minnesota-Kewaunee G&BW in one representative year received 37 percent of its interchange traffic from C&O and Ann Arbor boats, so its survival was a serious concern in ICC deliberations. In 1993, bereft since 1990 of its last carferry connection, GB&W was being courted to become part of Wisconsin Central, a newly created regional railroad that revived an old name.)

The abandonment decision was appealed twice and each time upheld, but petitions by protesting groups—the City of Milwaukee, the Board of Harbor Commissioners of the City of Milwaukee, the Michigan Department of Transportation, the United Transportation Union, the National Maritime Union, the Great Lakes Licensed Officers Organization, and the City of Ludington—led to stays for further administrative review.

Protestants claimed that C&O had driven away business—automobiles and people as well as freight—thus making the boats' unprofitability a self-fulfilling prophecy. Clearly, premeditated diversion of freight had taken place, but C&O's claim that it could move freight faster, more reliably, and at infinitely less cost on the all-rail

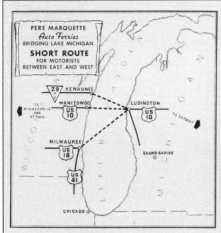

PASSENGER FARES AND AUTO RATES
BETWEEN ALL PORTS IN EITHER DIRECTION
(In effect every day)

ONE WAY $3.00
ROUND TRIP (Return Limit 90 Days)............. 5.25
ROUND TRIP (Return Limit 3 Days)............. 3.50
TAX NOT INCLUDED

MEALS AND BERTH EXTRA
BERTH RATES BETWEEN ALL PORTS
Berth . $1.50 Stateroom . $3.00 Stateroom Day Rate. . $1.50
AUTOMOBILE RATES BETWEEN ALL PORTS
One Way, any make or size......... $4.50 (Passengers Extra)
Round Trip, any make or size......... $7.50 (Passengers Extra)

INFORMATION
L. P. MESSMORE, Assistant General Passenger Agent
526-532 Grain and Stock Exchange, Milwaukee, Wis.
D. R. RATHSACK, General Agent Passenger Department
Pere Marquette Dock, Ludington, Mich.
F. A. YOUNG, General Passenger Agent
General Motors Building, Detroit, Mich.

The new streamlined City of Midland

CONSERVE YOUR CAR!

PERE MARQUETTE'S fast auto service between Ludington, Mich., and the Wisconsin ports of Milwaukee, Manitowoc, and Kewaunee, assists you to do your part in the national conservation of rubber and fuel. It's easier on you and your car when you take this time-saving "bridge" across Lake Michigan. You save gas and wear on tires, and at the same time enjoy a most delightful interlude in your trip.

Whole trains go aboard these great carferries. Without breaking bulk, freight moves on a direct straight short route across Lake Michigan *every day in the year*, serving shippers between the East and the Northwest. This means important hours saved and escape from congested areas. It means more "on-time" deliveries and more satisfied customers for you.

15M 3-42

SCHEDULES
and
FARES
PERE MARQUETTE RAILWAY
Auto Ferries
AAA

LUDINGTON · MILWAUKEE · MANITOWOC · KEWAUNEE

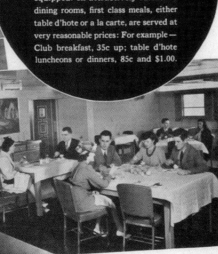

THE CRUISING comforts of a modern liner are provided on Pere Marquette Railway Autoferries. Perfect ventilation, hot and cold running water, soft, roomy berths are features of private staterooms. Wide decks beckon strollers, and public lounges are comfortably equipped. In attractively furnished dining rooms, first class meals, either table d'hote or a la carte, are served at very reasonable prices: For example — Club breakfast, 35c up; table d'hote luncheons or dinners, 85c and $1.00.

SCHEDULE OF DAILY SAILINGS
(Effective, March 5, 1942)

BETWEEN LUDINGTON AND MANITOWOC
WESTBOUND

Lv. Ludington (ET).................. 7:00 AM   5:30 PM
Ar. Manitowoc (CT)................. 10:00 AM   8:30 PM

EASTBOUND

Lv. Manitowoc (CT)................ 11:30 AM   10:00 PM
Ar. Ludington (ET).................. 4:30 PM ◆ 3:00 AM
◆ Passengers must disembark not later than 5:00 AM. E.T.

BETWEEN LUDINGTON AND MILWAUKEE
WESTBOUND

Lv. Ludington (ET)...4:15 AM 8:30 AM 1:00 PM 8:45 PM
Ar. Milwaukee
(Maple St.) (CT)...9:45 AM .... 6:30 PM ....
(Jones Island) (CT)......... 2:30 PM .... 2:00 AM

EASTBOUND

Lv. Milwaukee
(Maple St.) (CT)... 4:30 AM B   B   8:00 PM
(Jones Island) (CT)   A   12:00 noon 7:00 PM   A
Ar. Ludington (ET) ..12:00 noon 7:15 PM *3:00 AM 3:15 AM
A—Passengers and autos loaded only at Maple Street for the 4:30 AM and 8:00 PM departures.
B—Passengers and autos loaded only at Jones Island for 12:00 Noon and 7:00 PM departures.
* Passengers must disembark not later than 5:00 AM. E.T.

BETWEEN LUDINGTON AND KEWAUNEE
WESTBOUND

Lv. Ludington (ET)................... 5:00 AM   4:30 PM
Ar. Kewaunee (CT)................. 8:30 AM   8:00 PM

EASTBOUND

Lv. Kewaunee (CT)................. 9:30 AM †9:30 PM
Ar. Ludington (ET)................. 3:00 PM   3:00 AM
ET Eastern Standard Time. CT Central Standard Time.
†Daily except Sunday.

UNLESS OTHERWISE INDICATED PASSENGERS MUST DISEMBARK ON ARRIVAL, AND CANNOT BOARD BOATS UNTIL 30 MINUTES BEFORE LEAVING TIME. THOSE WITH AUTOS MUST BE AT THE DOCK AT LEAST 30 MINUTES BEFORE SCHEDULED SAILING TIME.

Pere Marquette Auto Ferries operate every day in the year.

In a March 1942 brochure, the year-old *City of Midland 41* gets all the attention.—C&O RAILWAY, C&O HISTORICAL SOCIETY collection

Above: With idler cars coupled to its pilot, a Pere Marquette 0-8-0 loads the *City of Midland 41* at Ludington. **Left:** The *City of Midland 41* was the first of the ferries to be designed to carry automobiles on its boat deck, driven up a curving ramp by crew members—as is clearly shown in this aerial view at Manitowoc, taken in 1955.—BOTH PHOTOS, C&O RAILWAY, C&O HISTORICAL SOCIETY COLLECTION

route was probably accurate. But the matter of passengers and automobiles was far more complicated, since driving around lake Michigan was in many cases a clearly inferior alternative to sailing across on a car ferry. Though the boats' original *raison d'etre* had been freight, changing times had made cars and people their primary purpose and public necessity.

The abandonment proceedings would drag on until they became the longest in the history of United States railroading. Meanwhile, C&O— officially Chessie System since 1973—attempted to cut its losses by reducing service in various ways. Winter operations became unscheduled

and were handled by a single vessel, which was supplemented by a second boat when timetable operations began on Memorial Day. August saw a third vessel in steam, allowing a pair of round-trips to Milwaukee and Manitowoc and one to Kewaunee.

In 1977, when Chessie had tried to get through the summer with just two boats and a consequently reduced schedule, a court order had required the full schedule for the month of August. Then, in 1979, Chessie again attempted to cancel the expanded sailings, this time on just two weeks' notice, and lay off the *Badger*'s crew, which had just been put in place preparatory to

This menu from 1968 devotes as much space to promoting the modern specifications of the *Badger* and *Spartan* as to listing the meals. The full fleet is impressively arrayed across the bottom.—WILLIAM F. HOWES JR. COLLECTION

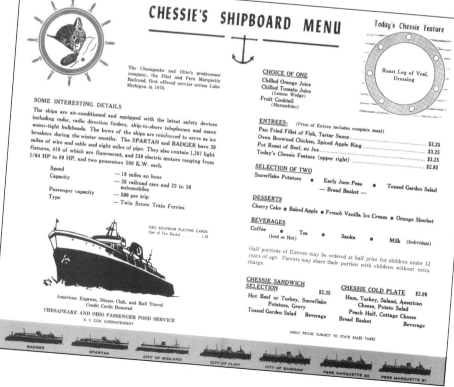

CHESSIE'S SHIPBOARD MENU

Today's Chessie Feature

Roast Leg of Veal, Dressing

The Chesapeake and Ohio's predecessor company, the Flint and Pere Marquette Railroad, first offered service across Lake Michigan in 1876.

SOME INTERESTING DETAILS

The ships are air-conditioned and equipped with the latest safety devices including radar, radio direction finders, ship-to-shore telephones and many water-tight bulkheads. The bows of the ships are reinforced to serve as ice breakers during the winter months. The SPARTAN and BADGER have 30 miles of wire and cable and eight miles of pipe. They also contain 1,387 light fixtures, 410 of which are fluorescent, and 330 electric motors ranging from 1/64 HP to 60 HP, and two generators 500 K.W. each.

Speed	— 18 miles an hour
Capacity	— 26 railroad cars and 25 to 50 automobiles
Passenger capacity	— 500 per trip
Type	— Twin Screw Train Ferries

C&O SOUVENIR PLAYING CARDS
(Set of Two Decks) 1.75

American Express, Diners Club, and Rail Travel Credit Cards Honored

CHESAPEAKE AND OHIO PASSENGER FOOD SERVICE
K. S. COX, SUPERINTENDENT

CHOICE OF ONE
Chilled Orange Juice
Chilled Tomato Juice
(Lemon Wedge)
Fruit Cocktail
(Maraschino)

ENTREES: *(Price of Entree includes complete meal)*
Pan Fried Fillet of Fish, Tartar Sauce
Oven Browned Chicken, Spiced Apple Ring $3.25
Pot Roast of Beef, au Jus $3.25
Today's Chessie Feature (upper right) $2.85

SELECTION OF TWO
Snowflake Potatoes • Early June Peas • Tossed Garden Salad
— Bread Basket —

DESSERTS
Cherry Cake • Baked Apple • French Vanilla Ice Cream • Orange Sherbet

BEVERAGES
Coffee • Tea • Sanka • Milk (Individual)
(Iced or Hot)

Half portions of Entrees may be ordered at half price for children under 12 years of age. Parents may share their portion with children without extra charge.

CHESSIE SANDWICH SELECTION $2.35
Hot Beef or Turkey, Snowflake Potatoes, Gravy
Tossed Garden Salad   Beverage

CHESSIE COLD PLATE $2.00
Ham, Turkey, Salami, American Cheese, Potato Salad
Peach Half, Cottage Cheese
Bread Basket   Beverage

MENU PRICES SUBJECT TO STATE SALES TAXES

BADGER   SPARTAN   CITY OF MIDLAND   CITY OF FLINT   CITY OF SAGINAW   PERE MARQUETTE 22   PERE MARQUETTE 21

Left: The car ferries loaded coal into their bunkers directly from hopper cars positioned on the car deck; this view of the process aboard *City of Midland 41* shows the hatches swung out of the way. **Above:** From the bunkers, the coal got to the fireboxes by way of automatic stokers—but under the watchful eye of the fireman, as shown here aboard the *Badger*.—Both photos, C&O Railway, C&O Historical Society collection

In their interiors, the *Badger* (shown here) and identical sister *Spartan* lacked the stylishness of predecessor *City of Midland 41*. In the dining room one family tackles enormous slabs of watermelon, while in an outside stateroom parents clad in chic bedtime attire read a bedtime story to their daughter.—Both photos, C&O Railway, C&O Historical Society collection

three-boat operation. This time the compromise was a full schedule on August weekends only—but all three boats did have fire in their bellies that summer. Then, sailings again became catch-as-catch-can in the winter, with a single boat hauling freight cars as needed between Ludington and the three Wisconsin ports.

The tug-of-war continued between Chessie, the states and municipalities, and the unions. The ICC's environmental impact statement said that the ferries' discontinuance would have drastic consequences for the port cities, where $7.2 million in annual tourist revenue and 13 percent of the existing jobs could be lost. Though the boats were expensive to fuel, coal was a non-critical resource, which might have been seen as a mark in their favor in those oil-short times. On the other hand, the boats' coal smoke violated state and local clean-air standards in Milwaukee, and the city had in fact fined the *Badger*—though not after her imperiled status became obvious, for Milwaukee didn't want to lose her and her sisters.

All those factors were weighed, along with such esoterica as this: The boats had been used extensively for lake-trout stocking, with about 40 percent of the fingerlings stocked each year being dropped mid-lake from hatchery trucks riding the C&O ferries.

In early 1980 Chessie offered to sell all three boats plus support facilities to the states of Michigan and Wisconsin for $20 million, then lease them back for $1. For its part the railroad agreed (subject to various provisions on cost-of-living increases and labor protection) to operate

Above: At Kewaunee, a pair of Green Bay & Western Alco RS3's switch the *Badger*, sister *Spartan* is at the right. Left: Sidelaunching the *Badger* at the Christy Corporation Shipyards in Sturgeon Bay.—BOTH PHOTOS, C&O RAILWAY, C&O HISTORICAL SOCIETY COLLECTION Below: Breakfast menu from 1968 was a simple affair.—WILLIAM F. HOWES JR. COLLECTION

two boats to Manitowoc and Kewaunee without subsidy for another decade. (Add an additional $3 million to the purchase price and C&O would throw in Milwaukee service as well.) State funds of this magnitude were unavailable, however. Meanwhile, the *Spartan*'s fires had been dropped for the last time in 1979, and C&O offered her for sale—"as is, where is, C&O Docks, Ludington," according to a brochure printed for the occasion, with bids due August 29, 1980.

Good Morning

CHESAPEAKE
AND OHIO
RAILWAY

CHESSIE SPECIAL
$1.00

Chilled Orange, Tomato or Prune Juice
Dry or Cooked Cereal with Milk
Toast, Dry or Buttered, Jelly
Coffee   Tea   Milk
Hot Chocolate   Sanka

Club Selection
$1.65

CHOICE OF ONE
Grapefruit Segments, Chilled Orange, Tomato or Prune Juice
Dry or Cooked Cereal with Milk

1. GRILLED SMOKED HAM OR SUGAR CURED BACON
WITH EGGS, ANY STYLE, BUTTERED TOAST, JELLY

2. WHEAT CAKES OR FRENCH TOAST WITH SYRUP,
SAUSAGE, BACON OR HAM

Coffee   Tea   Milk   Sanka   Hot Chocolate

American Express, Diners Club, and Rail Travel
Credit Cards Honored

C&O PASSENGER FOOD SERVICE
K. S. COX, Superintendent

Chessie's boats appeared doomed without state subsidies—which, in fact, Michigan had already begun providing for Ann Arbor's car ferries and for the *Chief Wawatam*. Eventually some subsidies did come Chessie's way: a $770,000 grant from Michigan to keep the Ludington-Milwaukee service running from the railroad's announced May 12 abandonment date through October 6, 1980—daily except Tuesday and Wednesday, but for passengers and automobiles only, no freight cars. That proved to be the end, however, and boats to Milwaukee's Jones Island stopped for good when the subsidies expired. Manitowoc service was the next to be abandoned, as the *Badger* sailed from that Wisconsin port for the last time (under Chessie auspices, it now must be added) on January 9, 1982.

That left just Kewaunee—the final victim of the ICC's 1978 "Kewaunee Package" compromise—and its agreed-upon demise, set for spring of 1983, was fast approaching. At the eleventh hour the cavalry appeared, in the guise of a group of Ludington-area businessmen led by Glen Bowden, a motel owner, and George Towns, a retired construction contractor. Under the auspices of the Michigan-Wisconsin Transportation Company, they agreed to purchase the three boats from Chessie (officially CSX since November 1980) for $3, lease the Ludington port facilities from the railroad, and assume labor-protection costs for six years—whether the boats sailed or not. In return, CSX agreed to continue cross-lake rail shipments for that period.

MWT was born on July 1, 1983, with the *City of Midland 41* offering Ludington-Kewaunee service—Thursday through Sunday at first, then daily. A week later the company steamed up the *Badger* to restore summer-only Ludington-Milwaukee service hauling automobiles and passengers only, an experiment that was terminated after the 1984 season. But right from the beginning it was clear that MWT was in for some heavy sledding, since operating costs for each boat were an estimated $18,000 per day, crew wages included. First-year losses were about $600,000—"not half as bad as we'd expected," according to Bowden.

Losses continued, but so did service—driven perhaps in part by the need to guarantee wages into 1989. Towns dropped out quickly, but Bowden pressed on, watching passenger traffic grow—to 83,500 in 1987 and 94,249 in 1988, along with 34,673 autos and 6,396 railroad cars.

Left: The *Spartan* by 1979 featured the Chessie emblem.— Karl Zimmermann
Below: The *Spartan* maneuvers in Milwaukee Harbor at Jones Island.—Russ Porter

Right: As part of the modernization program in the early 1950's, the *City of Saginaw 31* (seen booming across the lake) and *City of Flint 32* received the streamlined funnel introduced by the *City of Midland 41*. **Middle right:** Also as part of the modernization program, *Pere Marquette 21* and *Pere Marquette 22* were stretched and given conical funnels. No. 22 underwent this surgery at Manitowoc Shipbuilding in April of 1953. **Lower right:** The work completed, she smokes it up on the lake.—THREE PHOTOS, C&O RAILWAY, C&O HISTORICAL SOCIETY COLLECTION

These increases came in spite of on-again, off-again food service, sometimes reduced to nothing more than vending machines. The *City of Midland* sailed on the Ludingon-Kewaunee route until November 1988, when she was replaced by the *Badger* for MWT's final two years of operation. On November 16, 1990, the *Badger* made her last trip for MWT—perhaps because the channel at Kewaunee had grown too shallow and the vessel had hit bottom passing through, or perhaps because there was no money to pay fuel bills.

Then another savior appeared: Charles F. Conrad, a retired industrialist from Holland, Michigan, whose father had been chief engineer aboard Pere Marquette's car ferries. "Those ferries are a big part of my childhood," Conrad has said. Determined to step in and save their descendants, he purchased the three ex-C&O boats in July 1991—only to have the deal nullified four months later when Bowden declared bankruptcy and the courts seized the vessels.

Finally, in February 1992, the U. S. Bankruptcy Court awarded the three car ferries to Conrad's Lake Michigan Carferry Service and, on May 15, the company began summer-season Ludington-Manitowoc sailings with the *Badger*—returning service to a route discontinued a decade earlier. By the time LMCS ended a very

successful inaugural season on October 12, the *Badger* had carried some 115,000 passengers and 34,000 vehicles—far beyond projections.

Before returning to service, the boat had undergone some $500,000 in renovations that included fresh paint both inside and out; refurbishing of the 44 outside staterooms; replacement of the 16 inside staterooms by a gift shop, an exhibit area showcasing carferry history (created in cooperation with the Manitowoc Maritime Museum), a television/video room, and an arcade game room; enclosure under canopy of the after-boat deck (where autos used to be parked); and opening of a buffet-style restaurant on boat deck and a deli buffet on the spar deck.

Though Bowden realized the importance of passengers to MWT's success—by the end automobiles and people were 80 percent of the business, which was profitable in summer but lost money in winter—Conrad more successfully

catered to them. As a seasonal operation, non-union and out from under the complex and costly requirements of being a railroad (as MWT always was), Lake Michigan Carferry Service shows every sign of having a bright future.

"The ferries are part of Ludington," Conrad has said. "They've been on the lake for the past hundred years, and I want to do whatever I can to assure they'll be running for the next hundred."

Annie's Fleet

An Arbor's carferry operation across Lake Michigan was the first, dating back to November 27, 1892, when the link was forged between Frankfort and Kewaunee. In the late 1970's, when Annie's boats were going great guns, it seemed probable that the first would survive to be the last, but matters worked out to be otherwise.

It was *Ann Arbor No. 1* and *No. 2*, wooden-hulled vessels designed by noted naval architect Frank E. Kirby, that began it all. By the time that Toledo, Ann Arbor & Northern Michigan president James M. Ashley, a former Montana governor, approached Kirby about creating these pioneering cross-lake vessels, Kirby had some experience with car ferries, having designed the *Saint Ignace* in 1888 for Mackinac Transportation Company. Like this Straits of Mackinac vessel, Ann Arbor's ferries were wooden-hulled—oak, with steel sheathing to four feet above the water line—and had a bow propellor to facilitate ice-breaking. The TAA&NM vessels also had twin screws aft, with each propellor powered by its own engine, for a total of three. As built, the vessels' stacks, like their engines, were widely separated fore and aft.

The two sisters (*No. 2* was essentially identical to but just slightly larger than *No. 1*) were constructed at Craig Ship Building in Toledo.

Opposite: In this wintry view from early 1979, the *City of Milwaukee*—then leased to Ann Arbor—still wears Grand Trunk dress: wet-noodle "GT" on her bows, red-capped blue funnels.—Tom Post **Above:** The *Arthur K. Atkinson* forms an impressive backdrop for Ann Arbor diesels in this 1975 view at Elberta.—Michael Caramanna, John S. Ingles collection **Right:** On a frigid eastbound crossing of the lake in March 1979, the *City of Milwaukee* is paced by fleetmate *Viking*. **Below right:** *Viking*'s builder's plate.—Two photos, Joe McMillan

Each could carry 24 freight cars on four tracks, while the *Saint Ignace* carried only ten on two. But the most significant difference was that, while the *Saint Ignace* was a bow-loader, the Ann Arbor boats—designed for open water as opposed to the relatively serene Straits of Mackinac—were stern-loaders, as all subsequent cross-Michigan boats would be.

Car ferries were important to the Toledo, Ann Arbor & Northern Michigan from the year it reached the port of Frankfort—1892, though predecessor lines had begun building north from Toledo as early as 1870, and TAA&NM's own corporate roots go back as far as 1884. Throughout its history the Ann Arbor Railroad

Classic car ferries in winter ice provided a remarkable continuity—on Ann Arbor, a run of no less than 90 years. In these scenes from March 1979 at Kewaunee, the *Viking* (rebuilt from *Ann Arbor No. 7*, delivered in 1925) and, particularly, former Grand Trunk *City of Milwaukee* (1931) show timeless profiles and old-fashioned details.—THREE PHOTOS, JOE MCMILLAN

(as it became in 1895, in the wake of TAA&NM's bankruptcy) was basically a 292-mile main line connecting Toledo with cross-Lake Michigan boats at Frankfort, with the relatively important on-line university city of Ann Arbor generating some business too. By the time the carferry operations reached their peak, the mileage of the boat routes far exceeded that of the rail portion of AA.

The initial ferry route was from Frankfort to Kewaunee—"Where Rail and Water Meet," according to a sign at the station there—and connection with the Kewaunee, Green Bay & Western. In 1894 service was added to Menominee (interchanging with the Chicago, Milwaukee & St. Paul, Chicago & North Western, and Wisconsin & Michigan) on Michigan's Upper Peninsula, via the Sturgeon Bay Ship Canal and Green Bay, and in 1895 to Gladstone, also on the "U. P.," for interchange with the Soo Line. Because ice in Little Bay de Noc made Gladstone hard to reach in winter, service was shifted to Manistique—seasonally at first, then permanently, in 1902. In 1896, Manitowoc had been added, reaching the C&NW at a second point, and the Wisconsin Central, which later became part of the Soo Line.

Ann Arbor's maritime operations all funneled into the single port of Frankfort on Lake Michigan's east shore. Here Lake Betsie provided an outstandingly secure harbor, and the spirit and livelihood of the towns of Frankfort and Elberta—across the lake, the actual location of the AA's two slips and rail yards—became deeply enmeshed in the ethos of the car ferries.

Though the TAA&NM's carferry inaugural was hardly auspicious—No. 1 grounded near Kewaunee on her first westbound crossing—the service grew and other boats came on at regular intervals. *Ann Arbor No. 3*—steel-hulled, built in 1898 at Cleveland's Globe Iron Works, originally powered by the two bow engines removed from her elder sisters—survived in service a remarkable 62 years. A quite similar *No. 4* came from Globe in 1906.

Ann Arbor No. 5, another Kirby design, constructed in 1910 by Toledo Shipbuilding Company (after *No. 1* was destroyed by fire at Manitowoc), again set a new direction for AA boats, showing a profile with two stacks forward that was much like Robert Logan's designs for Pere Marquette. Big, powerful, a good ice-breaker, *No. 5* was also a trend-setter in being the first car ferry with a sea gate—a proven necessity after *Pere Marquette 18* foundered.

Ann Arbor No. 6 was built in 1917 by Great Lakes Engineering Works at Ecorse, Michigan. No. 7 was AA's member of Manitowoc Shipbuilding's sextet of classic sisters, shared with Grand Trunk and Pere Marquette. *Wabash*, which came in 1927 from Toledo Shipbuilding, was the last Ann Arbor newbuilding and the first of the line's boats to carry a name, honoring her

Text continued on page 44

Perhaps half a century earlier, *Ann Arbor No. 5* (foreground) and *No. 4* strike a similar but more desperate pose as the Frankfort townspeople come out to see the pair locked in ice.— STEAMSHIP HISTORICAL SOCIETY COLLECTION, UNIVERSITY OF BALTIMORE LIBRARY

Top: Dawn is just beginning to streak the night sky with purple as Chessie's *Spartan* (left) and Annie's *Arthur K. Atkinson* wait at Kewaunee.—Tom Post **Left:** *Ann Arbor No. 5* floats snug against the dock at Elberta in 1961. To this boat, constructed in 1910, goes the distinction of being the first car ferry to feature a sea gate.—John S. Ingles **Above:** Her sea gate raised, *No. 5* receives autos at Manistique, Michigan, in 1964. Ann Arbor dropped service to this Upper Peninsula port in 1968.—John S. Ingles collection

Above left: In the *Viking*'s wheelhouse, attention is focused on a lake locked in midsummer fog. **Left:** The dining room aboard the *Viking* was unassuming but cozy. The specials of the day were beef pot roast, chop suey with rice, and Polish sausage and sauerkraut.—Two photos, Karl Zimmermann **Above:** *Viking*'s nameplate encapsulated her history.—Joe McMillan **Below:** Ensconsed in the port facilities of Lake Betsie, the *Viking* waits to load railcars, automobiles, and passengers as dawn light casts a melancholy blue glow on Frankfort and Elberta. Lake Michigan in the distance appears serene on this August day in 1976.—Robert E. Mohowski

ANN ARBOR RAILROAD   ANN ARBOR RAILROAD

THE SHORTEST
AUTO ROUTE
ACROSS LAKE MICHIGAN

SIX LARGE
MODERN STEEL
STEAMSHIPS
CARRYING AUTOMOBILES & TOURISTS

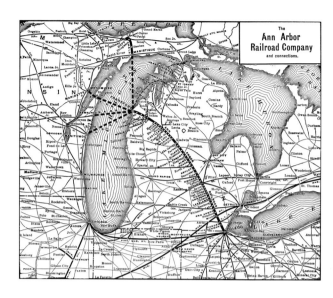

The
Ann Arbor
Railroad Company
and connections.

Ann Arbor's 1930 brochure features the relatively new *Wabash* (1927) on the cover, while the map inside shows AA's wide range of routes across Lake Michigan. On the outside back cover of the brochure, the fleet photographs are wildly misidentified with the same photo of *No. 5* shown twice—as *No. 3* and *No. 6*—and a photo of *No. 6* run twice and identified as *No. 4* and *No. 5*.—STEVE ELVE COLLECTION

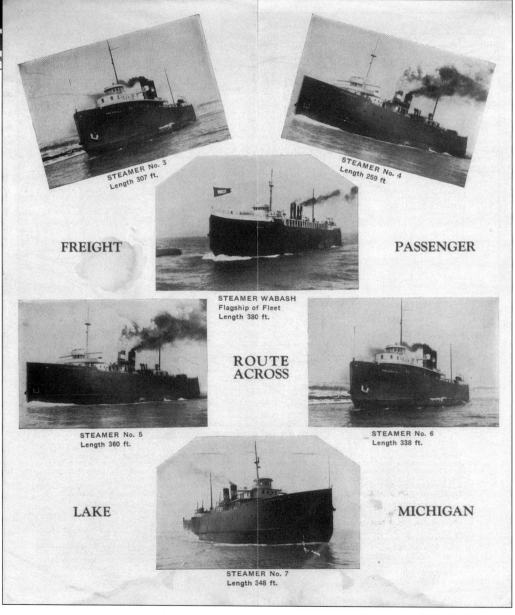

STEAMER No. 3
Length 307 ft.

STEAMER No. 4
Length 259 ft.

FREIGHT

PASSENGER

STEAMER WABASH
Flagship of Fleet
Length 380 ft.

ROUTE
ACROSS

STEAMER No. 5
Length 360 ft.

STEAMER No. 6
Length 338 ft.

LAKE

MICHIGAN

STEAMER No. 7
Length 348 ft.

Left: *Ann Arbor No. 1*—seen here at the slip at Kewaunee—inaugurated Lake Michigan carferry service in November 1892. —STEVE ELVE COLLECTION

Above: *Ann Arbor No. 3* steams into Betsie Lake, swinging to make a landing at the east slip, while No. 5 waits at the west slip. **Left:** *Ann Arbor No. 7*—one of Manitowoc Shipbuilding's handsome sextet—steams away from the east slip at Elberta. —BOTH PHOTOS, STEVE ELVE COLLECTION

Car ferries in early postcards

Left: *Ann Arbor No. 3* bucks the ice-packed entrance to the harbor at Frankfort in the teens. **Below:** Grand Trunk's first boat, the *Grand Haven* of 1903. Location is probably Grand Haven, Michigan.—BOTH, STEVE ELVE COLLECTION

Carferry Route operating between Milwaukee and Grand Haven.

GRAND TRUNK RAILWAY SYSTEM

GRAND TRUNK LINE.

S.S. WABASH   FRANKFORT, MICH.

Above and right:
The *Wabash* of 1927—AA's last newbuilding, and the first boat to carry a name rather than a number—is seen at Frankfort and docking at Manistique. Both views date from the 1930's.—BOTH PHOTOS, STEVE ELVE COLLECTION

©L.L. Cook Co. 1938
MILWAUKEE, WIS.

Opposite: In this view across Betsie Lake, the soft light of dawn touches the different profiles of the *Arthur K. Atkinson* (left in photo) and the *City of Milwaukee*.
—KARL ZIMMERMANN

Above: Sporting Ann Arbor's distinctive funnel marking—which worked even better with twin-stackers, yielding "A-A"—*No. 3* lays down a trail of smoke crossing the lake. Unique among AA vessels in having a double hull, she enjoyed a long and successful career, sailing until 1960.—Steamship Historical Society collection, University of Baltimore Library

Right: The ice-covered decks and wheelhouse of *Ann Arbor No. 3* show just how fierce winter on the lakes can be. The car ferries' ice-breaking ability set them apart from other Great Lakes vessels, which simply go into lay-up in the dead of winter—a luxury not allowed boats that toted railcars.—Manitowoc Maritime Museum, Manitowoc, Wisconsin **Below:** Between 1894 and 1906, the railroad changed names—and flagships, from *Ann Arbor No. 2* to *Ann Arbor No. 3*.—Both passes, Steve Elve collection

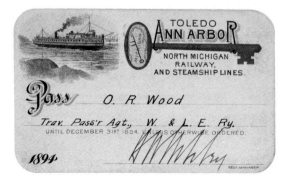

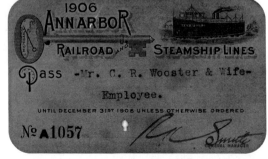

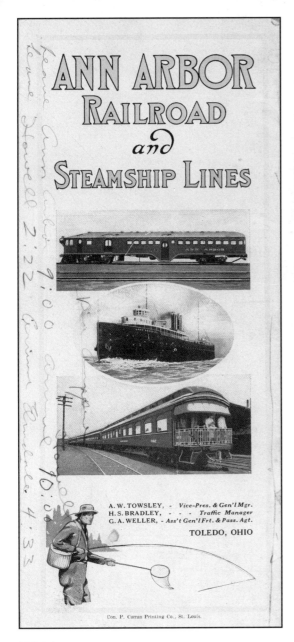

Left: This early timetable featured the motorcars that plied AA's Toledo-Owosso and Owosso-Cadillac lines, as well as car ferry *No. 5* and the mainline trains with "Pullman Drawing Room Sleeping Cars" and "Cafe-Parlor Cars" to Frankfort, Elberta, and "Boat Landing"—all listed as 292 miles from Toledo. Carferry competitor Pere Marquette teamed up to provide through sleeper service from Chicago. **Top:** In this view looking from Elberta across Betsie Lake toward Frankfort, *Ann Arbor No. 1* is moored next to near-identical sister *No. 2*. **Above:** *Ann Arbor No. 2* is heavily laden with passengers as she enters the Menominee River at Menominee, Michigan. **Below:** Seen from broadside, *Ann Arbor No. 3* was lean and lanky.—ALL ILLUSTRATIONS, STEVE ELVE COLLECTION

Ann Arbor No. 6 had been laid down at Great Lakes Engineering Works as *Maitland No. 2* for the Toronto, Hamilton & Buffalo Navigation Company. AA had chartered sister *Maitland No. 1*, had liked her, and thus had decided to purchase *No. 2*, already under construction. Here she steams for AA on Lake Michigan—rather than Lake Erie, as had been intended when her keel was laid.—STEAMSHIP HISTORICAL SOCIETY COLLECTION, UNIVERSITY OF BALTIMORE LIBRARY

Continued from page 35
owner, the railroad that then controlled Ann Arbor.

After this came a period of stability that stretched over decades; though *Ann Arbor No. 4* was sold in 1937, the other five steel-hulled vessels steamed on, sailing from Frankfort to Manitowoc, Kewaunee, Menominee, and Manistique. "These ships are built to carry railroad cars from point to point," according to a 1930 brochure, "but are equipped with comfortable, modern passenger accommodations. This equipment includes cabins, state-rooms, dining rooms, radio, and all other modern conveniences for the safety and comfort of travelers. These ships do not operate upon fixed schedule, however, a boat leaves Frankfort for each of the ports of call at least once every twenty-four hours and at times this service is more frequent."

Ann Arbor's 1957 brochure looked remarkably like the one from 1930.

From the six ferries of 1930, however, the number of active boats eventually shrank to one. Stalwart vessel of Annie's latter years was the new-old *Viking*, and to her would fall the bittersweet honor of ending AA service in April of 1982, just over a decade short of the century mark. Her latter-day consorts were the somewhat star-crossed *Arthur K. Atkinson* and the Grand Trunk's elegant *City of Milwaukee*.

Viewed aesthetically, the story of the Michigan car ferries in twilight centered on the *City of Milwaukee*. Truly the lady of the lake in her last years under steam, this venerable, graceful beauty had come to the Grand Trunk Milwaukee Car Ferry Company from Manitowoc

Shipbuilding in 1931, the last of six identical sisters: *Pere Marquette 21* and *22* (1924); *Ann Arbor No. 7* (1925), which at age forty would be rebuilt as the *Viking*; and *Grand Rapids* (1926), *Madison* (1927), and *City of Milwaukee* for the GT.

The *City of Milwaukee* was built to replace the *Milwaukee*, which had sunk on October 22, 1929, with the loss of all hands. (The ill-fated *Milwaukee*, built in 1903 for the Manistique, Marquette & Northern's unsuccessful and evanescent carferry operations, was acquired by Grand Trunk in 1908). The words "City of" were a conscious addition in the new boat's name, intended for differentiation from her doomed predecessor. The Grand Trunk's three sisters were changed little over the years, though they were converted to oil firing in 1947, allowing a ten-man reduction in each crew.

The *City of Milwaukee* was available for Ann Arbor service because the Grand Trunk had succeeded where Chessie up to that point had failed. On 1978, the Interstate Commerce Commission finally ruled favorably on GT's abandonment petition of February 14, 1975, allowing the railroad to terminate in November the carferry service that had linked Muskegon, Michigan, with Milwaukee since 1933—and was currently piling up losses claimed to be in excess of $1 million annually. (When Grand Trunk Milwaukee Car Ferry Company had begun service back in 1903, the Michigan port had been Grand Haven—and the line's first vessel, appropriately, the *Grand Haven*. The switch to Muskegon occured when the Pennsylvania Railroad became a partner in the operation.) The "Trunkers" had never carried automobiles and had ended their

Car Ferry № 1
Manistique, Marquette and Northern.

limited passenger service in 1971, so they were less visible than Chessie's boats and perhaps for that reason less strenuously supported.

In November 1978 the State of Michigan leased the *City of Milwaukee* to operate on the Ann Arbor routes and later, on May 18, 1979, purchased her for $2, at the same time waiving rights to the *Madison*; GT had sold the *Grand Rapids* earlier—though in fact both those vessels actually remained on Muskegon Lake until 1989, when they were towed away after plans to convert them to a floating hotel and convention center at Grand Haven's Harbor Island finally fizzled.

For the Ann Arbor as for the GT, the *City of Milwaukee* had just a freight "ticket," or certificate, from the Coast Guard and thus could carry no more than a dozen passengers. Passenger boats required more extensive,

expensive life-saving equipment, cost more to insure, and were forbidden to carry gasoline, propane and other flammables permitted on freight boats.

One such passenger boat was the *Viking*, which had come from Manitowoc Shipbuilding as *Ann Arbor No. 7* in 1925 and was thus actually six years older than sister *City of Milwaukee*. She began her new life as the *Viking* in 1965 when—at a cost of $2.8 million, $2.5 million of which was loaned by the Detroit, Toledo & Ironton, which at that time controlled AA—she was dieselized and modernized. With the installation of four 16-cylinder Electro-Motive Division diesels, her top speed increased from 14 to 21 miles per hour, making her the fastest car ferry on the lake. She was given a bow thruster—common among Great Lakes freighters and, now,

Above, right, and below right: Grand Trunk Milwaukee Car Ferry Company's classic three sisters: *Grand Rapids* (Steve Elve collection), *Madison,* and the *City of Milwaukee* (Both, Steamship Historical Society collection, University of Baltimore Library).

among seagoing vessels but always unique to the *Viking* among car ferries—which proved a great help in maneuvering in close quarters and docking. Her passenger deck was raised, providing the extra clearance on the car deck necessary for "high and wide" freight cars.

The two slender, raked funnels—to the end a part of the *City of Milwaukee*'s classic profile—were replaced aboard No. 7 by a single broad, tapered stack, and the wheelhouse was rebuilt. The passenger quarters were modernized: An enlarged forward observation lounge commandeered much of the space originally alloted to staterooms, only four of which remained, along with a sitting room adjoining one of them that was used by company officials when they were aboard. In later years blue paint covered all the wood paneling in the passenger area, and other changes altered the ambiance in the direction of modernity.

Many Ann Arbor men considered No. 7 their best boat, and in her reincarnation as the *Viking* she continued that tradition of reliable, sustained service. For years she was Annie's only boat, after the *Arthur K. Atkinson*—the first of the Ann Arbor rebuilds, completed in 1959—was laid up with a cracked crankshaft in 1973.

The *AKA* had entered service in 1917 as Ann Arbor No. 6, a boat actually designed for Toronto, Hamilton & Buffalo Navigation Company rather than Ann Arbor and, maybe at least partly for that reason, plagued with trouble from the start. Perhaps that is why her rebuilding, done by Manitowoc Shipbuilding, was extensive—much more so, for instance, than the *Viking*'s or the *City of Green Bay*'s. (The latter occured in 1962 and simply involved taking the 1927 *Wabash* and raising her spar deck, converting her to oil firing, and giving her a new funnel.)

To create the *Arthur K. Atkinson*, No. 6 was lengthened by 34 feet, had her spar deck raised two feet, and was equipped with a pair of 2,750-h.p. Nordberg non-reversing diesels with variable-pitch propellers. She received a new pilot house and stack, both very much in the streamlined mode, had her superstructure altered toward sleekness, and was named for the president of the Wabash, which then controlled the Ann Arbor. When she returned to service on March 14, 1959, after $2,305,000 had been spent on her renewal, even No. 6's close friends would have had a hard time recognizing her.

Apparently No. 6's devils were not exorcised, however, as the *Arthur K. Atkinson* fell short of perfection. For one thing, steam was still needed for heat, deck machinery, and steering. More serious were the problems that developed with the variable-pitch propellors when they proved susceptible to breaking in ice—a true Achilles' heel for a Lake Michigan car ferry, which spent

THE "ARTHUR K. ATKINSON"

THE ANN ARBOR RAILROAD COMPANY
STEAMSHIPS
DINING ROOM SERVICE
BREAKFAST

No. 1   **$.60**

Fruit or Fruit Juice
Buttered Toast or Sweet Rolls with Jelly
Coffee   Tea   Milk

No. 2   **$.90**

Fruit or Fruit Juice
Cereal (Dry or Cooked) with Cream
Buttered Toast or Sweet Rolls with Jelly
Coffee   Tea   Milk

No. 3   **$1.40**

Fruit or Fruit Juice
Eggs - Fried or Scrambled (2), or
Bacon or Sausage with Cakes
Buttered Toast
Coffee   Tea   Milk

No. 4   **$1.65**

Fruit Juice or Cereal
Bacon, Ham or Sausage with Eggs & Buttered Toast
Preserves
Coffee   Tea   Milk

PARENTS MAY SHARE THEIR PORTIONS WITH CHILDREN WITHOUT EXTRA CHARGE, OR HALF PORTIONS AT HALF PRICE WILL BE SERVED TO CHILDREN UNDER 12 YEARS OF AGE.

2-60

many months a year negotiating ice-bound waters. The *coup de grace* came in 1973, and she was laid up at Frankfort.

At that time the Ann Arbor undoubtedly had been just as glad to see the *AKA* tied up, for the railroad was bankrupt (having defaulted on the DT&I's loan for the *Viking*'s conversion) and had requested permission from the ICC to abandon all ferry operations. After the *AKA*'s crippling, the Ann Arbor embargoed the route to Manitowoc—which the ICC had refused to let them abandon the previous year, in response to an earlier petition, filed jointly with C&O. Two other long-time Ann Arbor routes from Frankfort had already been abandoned—to Manistee in 1968, and to Menominee in 1970—and the *City of Green Bay* was out of the picture, her certificate allowed to expire in 1972.

With the *Arthur K. Atkinson* down, that left

The *AKA* was newly minted when she offered this breakfast menu to her patrons in 1960.—STEVE ELVE COLLECTION

The facelift that in 1959 transformed dowdy *Ann Arbor No. 6* into the modernistic *Arthur K. Atkinson* was a major one, amply illustrated in these two profiles. **Right:** Number 6 in her as-built appearance.—STEAMSHIP HISTORICAL SOCIETY COLLECTION, UNIVERSITY OF BALTIMORE LIBRARY **Below right:** The sleekness of the *AKA* is evident as she rests during her seven years of lay-up in the 1970's.—KARL ZIMMERMANN

just the *Viking* shuttling the 64 miles between Frankfort and Kewaunee. Then came plans for Conrail, which carried with them the almost certain demise of the entire Ann Arbor, not just its boats. Finally, just in the nick of time, the State of Michigan appeared and saved Annie from her apparent fate. It was a rescue possible only with the expenditure of taxpayer dollars and as such was fragile. In 1977 the railroad (including the car ferries) was bought by the state and leased to Michigan Interstate, a private firm, for operation.

So as the 1970's drew to a close, it was very much "red sky at night" for Annie's boats. Service was extended again to Manitowoc on an as-needed basis. Clever, trendy brochures aimed at motorists touted "Your Lake Michigan Short Cut Between Michigan and Wisconsin." With truckers targeted as a potentially lucrative market, the number of tractor-trailer rigs conveyed in May through June 1980 climbed to 251, as opposed to just 60 the year before, while the passenger count for the same period rose to 9,157 from 6,343. (Freight cars were down 11 percent, to 4,117, however. Putting that in perspective, 80,272 freight cars had been carried back in 1925.)

Then along came the *City of Milwaukee* to enjoy a second life, as an Ann Arbor boat. Even the black-sheep *Arthur K. Atkinson* was prepared for a long-delayed return to service; in fall of 1979, her 38-ton port engine was lifted out and sent for repair to Cooper Bessemer (Nordberg's successor) in Grove City, Pennsylvania. On July

Above: At home in icy environs, the *City of Milwaukee* steams into port at Frankfort on March 11, 1979. **Left:** Undoubtedly the temperature is much warmer in the bowels of the *City*, where the chief engineer tends to the steam rudder engine.—BOTH PHOTOS, JOE MCMILLAN

Below: In a flashy dress worn only briefly for her own funeral, the *Viking* arrives at Frankfort on July 18, 1981, less than a year before the end.—STEVE ELVE **Right:** The Viking's ice-encrusted decking is emblematic of the year-round operations required of car ferries.—TOM POST

With a plume to show that she remained steam-powered (though now burning oil rather than coal), the *Wabash*—still carrying that name—sported a new funnel after her 1962 rebuilding into the *City of Green Bay.*—STEAMSHIP HISTORICAL SOCIETY COLLECTION, UNIVERSITY OF BALTIMORE LIBRARY

The AKA, for sale like a used car.—STEVE ELVE COLLECTION

22, 1980, the *Atkinson* sailed once more, leaving Frankfort under her own power for drydocking in South Chicago for hull inspection. Roughly a month later she was back in service, relegating the *City of Milwaukee* to the role of stand-by vessel for the rest of her career.

Then the castle, built on a foundation of state subsidies, began to crumble. On October 1, 1981, Michigan slashed its support of freight railroads by 35 percent, while announcing a plan to end all subsidies within five years. Finally, on April 26, 1982, Michigan Interstate halted all service north of the city of Ann Arbor because of high subsidy levels—a reported cumulative expenditure of $84 million. This shut-down included the car ferries. While temporary subsidies revived the trains for a time, the boats never sailed again.

Purchased by Peterson Builders, Inc., a shipyard in Sturgeon Bay, Wisconsin, the *Viking* left Frankfort under tow in May 1983, and the *Arthur K. Atkinson* followed her roughly one year later. Happily, the *City of Milwaukee*—designated a National Historic Landmark—has been preserved. Sold by the state to the City of Frankfort for $1, she was towed across Lake Betsie in December 1983 to a temporary home in Frankfort.

Subsequently turned over to the non-profit Society for the Preservation of the *City of Milwaukee*, she is again moored at Elberta, traditional haunt of Annie's boats, where she faces a still-problematic future as a museum vessel. Her enshrinement is appropriate, since many observers feel that she and her five Manitowoc Shipbuilding sisters represent the pinnacle of carferry design.

Elberta and Frankfort relied heavily on the Ann Arbor and its boats for both their livelihood and community pride, as suggested by the lighthouse-inspired gateway, topped with a model of the *Viking*, that marks the entrance to Frankfort.—ROGER COOK

Your Lake Michigan Short Cut
Between Michigan and Wisconsin

ann arbor railroad system
Ann Arbor Car Ferry
1979 Summer Car Ferry Schedule
Effective May 30 – Sept. 16

ANN ARBOR RAILROAD CARFERRY SCHEDULE

FRANKFORT, MICH.

TO

MANITOWOC, WISC.

KEWAUNEE, WISC.

MENOMINEE, MICH.

1968 SUMMER SCHEDULE
Effective June 8
thru September 8, 1968

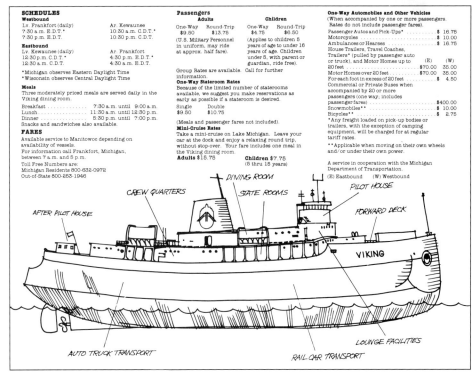

SCHEDULES

Westbound
Lv. Frankfort (daily)	Ar. Kewaunee
7:30 a.m. E.D.T.*	10:30 a.m. C.D.T.
7:30 p.m. E.D.T.	10:30 p.m. C.D.T.

Eastbound
Lv. Kewaunee (daily)	Ar. Frankfort
12:30 p.m. C.D.T.*	4:30 p.m. E.D.T.
12:30 a.m. C.D.T.	4:30 a.m. E.D.T.

*Michigan observes Eastern Daylight Time
*Wisconsin observes Central Daylight Time

Meals
Three moderately priced meals are served daily in the Viking dining room.

Breakfast	7:30 a.m. until 9:00 a.m.
Lunch	11:30 a.m. until 12:30 p.m.
Dinner	5:30 p.m. until 7:00 p.m.

Snacks and sandwiches also available.

FARES
Available service to Manitowoc depending on availability of vessels.
For information call Frankfort, Michigan, between 7 a.m. and 5 p.m.
Toll Free Numbers are:
Michigan Residents 800-632-0972
Out-of-State 800-253-1946

Passengers

Adults		Children	
One-Way	Round-Trip	One-Way	Round-Trip
$9.50	$13.75	$4.75	$6.50

(U.S. Military Personnel in uniform, may ride at approx. half fare).

(Applies to children 5 years of age to under 16 years of age. Children under 5, with parent or guardian, ride free).

Group Rates are available. Call for further information.

One-Way Stateroom Rates
Because of the limited number of staterooms available, we suggest you make reservations as early as possible if a stateroom is desired.

Single	Double
$9.50	$10.75

(Meals and passenger fares not included).

Mini-Cruise Rates
Take a mini-cruise on Lake Michigan. Leave your car at the dock and enjoy a relaxing round trip, without stop-over. Your fare includes one meal in the Viking dining room.
Adults $15.75   Children $7.75 (5 thru 15 years)

One-Way Automobiles and Other Vehicles
(When accompanied by one or more passengers. Rates do not include passenger fares).

	(E)	(W)
Passenger Autos and Pick-Ups*		$ 16.75
Motorcycles		$ 10.00
Ambulances or Hearses		$ 16.75
House Trailers, Travel Coaches, Trailers* (pulled by passenger auto or truck), and Motor Homes up to 20 feet	$70.00	35.00
Motor Homes over 20 feet	$70.00	35.00
For each foot in excess of 20 feet		$ 4.50
Commercial or Private Buses when accompanied by 20 or more passengers (one way; includes passenger fares)		$400.00
Snowmobiles**		$ 10.00
Bicycles**		$ 2.75

* Any freight loaded on pick-up bodies or trailers, with the exception of camping equipment, will be charged for at regular tariff rates.

** Applicable when moving on their own wheels and/or under their own power.

A service in cooperation with the Michigan Department of Transportation.

(E) Eastbound   (W) Westbound

Ann Arbor's carferry brochures went from the simply expository, in 1968, to the playfully trendy, in 1979. The latter featured a diagram and a description of nautical terms for the neophyte carferry passenger.—BOTH BROCHURES, STEVE ELVE COLLECTION

Mackinac Miracle:
the Chief Wawatam

3

The *Chief Wawatam*'s history is perhaps the most remarkable of the Great Lakes car ferries yet arguably the simplest. She began work in October of 1911 on the Straits of Mackinac, toting freight cars from Mackinaw City, on Michigan's Lower Peninsula, to St. Ignace, on the Upper Peninsula—then went right on doing just that until her retirement in 1984.

Say you were in the *Chief*'s pilothouse in her last years. Though it was the 1980's, it could as well have been seven decades earlier, aside from the presence of the enormous, arching Mackinac Bridge (opened in 1957) that loomed through the mist to the west and the cut of the pleasure craft that buzzed about. You would have been struck

by the peace and stillness of this ivory tower high atop the vessel, though below decks, in contrast, substantial sweat and clamor would have been occuring to move that whale of a boat across the Straits at eleven miles per hour.

But topside everything seemed in slow motion. The last of an infinite succession of coats of white paint was peeling off the wooden superstructure, though the brass in the pilothouse shown like new: the engine-room telegraphs ("Chadburns," in Great Lakes parlance, after their manufacturer); the handle of the whistle-pull; and the archaic, air-activated gauges that indicated the propeller direction (as well as the place of the *Chief*'s birth, by being inscribed "Toledo Shipbuilding Co."). Captain

Roderick J. Graham—the *Chief*'s final master, who took over in February 1974—was casual in a sport shirt with open collar, and hospitable. Working with a calm authority, he called out landmarks and commands in a quiet voice to the wheelsman, who responded with a spin of the enormous wheel, so tall he could easily have rested his chin on it had he cared to.

Just a few steps down from the pilothouse was the Hurricane Deck, where brass tags over doors identified the quarters of masters, mates, and engine-room officers. Earlier in her career, the *Chief Wawatam* had been an around-the-clock operation, with officers and crew living on board and standing alternating watches in the traditional maritime fashion. Though it had been

Opposite and center right: The *Chief* arrives at Mackinaw City.—KARL ZIMMERMANN **Top:** The *Chief* and a Soo Line locomotive—on a curious Straits-side turntable—at St. Ignace in the spring of 1973.—RUSS PORTER **Above:** Loading the *Chief* at St. Ignace—HOANG CHI COOK **Right:** Firing the *Chief*.—TOM POST

years since carloadings had been high enough to justify more than a single shift for the *Chief*—and even that inconsistent and infrequent in her final years—the boat's configuration exposed her heritage as an around-the-clock steamer, and as a passenger-carrier, too.

Unlike Annie's and Chessie's boats, the *Chief Wawatam* never catered aggressively to the substantial automobile traffic that could have come her way. In fact, operator Mackinac Transportation Company actually discouraged it, at first by treating automobiles as freight—loading them on flat cars, draining their gas tanks, levying freight tariffs—and later simply by charging high rates. Some passengers were transported, however, and the *Chief* for years carried the coaches of the *Lake Superior Limited*, operated by the Duluth, South Shore & Atlantic, which became part of the Soo Line. This train, a daylight accommodation run in spite of its grand name, made up in Mackinaw City, was ferried across the Straits by the *Chief*, and ran on DSS&A rails to Marquette, on the Upper Peninsula. In 1955 the train was transformed to a Budd Car originating in St. Ignace, and the *Chief* was out of the picture, except to carry connecting

foot passengers. The train was gone entirely less than three years later, and all passenger service on the *Chief* ceased about this time.

Though the space was all empty and superfluous in the vessel's final decades, the visitor who walked down the companionway to the Texas deck, once the passengers' domain, could easily identify the spacious dining room, window-lined and bright from a clerestory, where patrons of the *Lake Superior Limited* might have enjoyed breakfast or dinner. The mirrored buffet remained to the end, as did the circular, silvered radiator at the room's center. Forward was the observation lounge and the purser's window, where passengers once purchased their tickets. The entire deck was a floating ghost town.

Down deep in the ship's bowels, below the car deck, were the engine room, boilers, and stokehold. Here flesh-and-blood humans, not ghosts, were very much in evidence, performing age-old tasks. In the engine room, assistant engineer and oiler, alerted by a clattering bell, responded to the instructions telegraphed from the bridge and hauled on the throttles to put the great boat in motion. Then came the wonderfully mesmerizing, ryhthmic "*thunk*, chunk, *thunk*,

The *Chief Wawatam* approaches the slip at St. Ignace on a warm July day in 1979.
—KARL ZIMMERMANN

Above left: The *Chief*'s pilothouse and Texas deck are a memorial to traditional ways. **Above:** The slip at Saint Ignace is framed in the pilothouse window. **Far left:** "Chadburns" stand ready to relay the captain's commands to the engine room. **Left:** The ever-present life preservers are, thankfully, almost never used. **Below left and below:** While the wheelsman steadies a wheel almost as tall as he, Captain Roderick Graham studies the Straits through an open window.—ALL PHOTOS, KARL ZIMMERMANN

CHIEF WAWATAN, RAILWAY FERRY

DETROIT PUBLISHING CO.

U.S. MAIL
RAILWAY FERRY
CHIEF WAWATAN

Life on the Straits—in postcards

Top: The original *Sainte Marie* caught in ice. **Middle:** The *Chief Wawatam*, still designated as a carrier of the U.S. Mail. **Bottom:** The second *Sainte Marie*, with the *Chief* in the distance—ALL, STEVE ELVE COLLECTION

Steamer "Sainte Marie" Plying Straits of Mackinac, Mich.

1B-H2528

In the former officers' dining room, a single table and a few chairs sufficed for the crew's lunchbox meals after the galley, which provided three meals a day when the *Chief* was a round-the-clock operation, closed down for good in 1966.—Roger Cook

chunk" of falling connecting rods and thrusting pistons. There was warmth, the hiss of steam, the good aroma of hot grease—an olio of smells and sounds that typified the engine rooms of boats powered by reciprocating steam.

The stokehold was typical, too—of 1911. It was unheard-of in the 1980's. On a mid-summer afternoon, just three of the *Chief*'s six boilers would be fired, allowing the other three to be down for annual cleaning and inspection. For most of the year, four boilers in steam was standard operating procedure, but in winter the *Chief* fired all six for maximum power in ice-breaking. Three lanky youths, naked to the waist, were draped over metal shelf seats or in companionways, resting, seemingly asleep. Then, as the needles on the big steam gauges on the bulkhead dropped below 185 pounds of pressure, the firemen stirred and went to work, one at a time on the cramped deck.

A firebox door was opened, and the dusk of the room was flooded with a sudden dawn—a palpable wave of heat and blinding light. The fireman thrust his long-handled rake into the fire, making adjustments within the raging inferno, then went to the bunker, dug a scoopful of coal from below the restraining boards, and flung it deep into the firebox. (When the bunkers were full, no coal-passer was necessary; when the supply got low, an extra hand was hired to do

that job.) Again and again came the rasp of shovel and the uncoiling of muscle that sent the coal spraying deep into the belly of the firebox. Each of the three stokers took his turn; then the needles on the gauges rose again, the men slumped back into their torpid near-sleep, and all was quiet for a time in the fireroom.

If a "hand-bomber" such as the *Chief Wawatam* was an incredible rarity in the 1980's, she was of course the standard back in 1888 when car ferries began crossing the Straits of Mackinac. In that year, the Mackinac Transportation Company's *Saint Ignace* had initiated carferry service from her namesake city on the Upper Peninsula to Mackinaw City, on the Lower, getting the jump on cross-Lake Michigan service by four years. This wooden hulled pioneer had just two tracks, placed outboard of her cabin—a design never to be repeated—and thus could carry only ten railroad cars. In 1893 she was joined by a second boat, the *Sainte Marie*; with three tracks (for a capacity of eighteen cars) carried inside her superstructure, she forecast the two "modern" Mackinac Transportation boats.

In 1911 came the *Chief Wawatam*, the company's first steel-hulled vessel. She was designed by Frank E. Kirby, who had also been responsible for the two earlier ferries. The *Chief* was much the same size and had much in

common with the cross-Lake Michigan vessels being built at the time; this was not surprising, since Kirby also had designed *Ann Arbor Nos. 1* and *2* (in 1892) and *Ann Arbor No. 5* (in 1910). However, the *Chief* was linked to the two predecessor boats in Mackinac Transportation's fleet in being a bow-loader; this design characteristic, impossible for the cross-lake boats because of the high seas they faced, was workable in the Straits of Mackinac and made berthing easier.

Chief Wawatam, the vessel's namesake, was a Chippewa leader who is remembered in the writings of the 18th Century Engishman Alexander Henry, a trader in the Straits area who was befriended and eventually saved by Wawatam. Both the sound and sense of the word "Wawatam" are elusive; it apparently means "reflections," as in "flashes of light." And while Native American pronunciation seems to fall lightly on the second syllable, the men who worked aboard the *Chief Wawatam*—when they didn't simply call their vessel "the *Chief*"—

generally accented the first: "*Wah*-wah-tam."

The *Chief* had three screws, one forward and two aft. This bow propellor—an unusual and important aspect of her design, shared by her two predecessors as well as Kirby's Ann Arbor boats—proved very successful in ice-breaking. Not only did it provide additional power, it also pulled water out from under the ice, allowing it to crack more readily as the bow rode out on it, the typical method by which car ferries broke ice.

Chief Wawatam was a superb ice-breaker, one of the best ever on the lakes, but even better was the second *Sainte Marie*, which entered service in 1913. Also designed by Kirby, this boat appeared a stubby version of the *Chief* and was in fact considerably smaller, carrying only 14 freight cars compared to the *Chief*'s 26. The first *Sainte Marie*, wooden-hulled like the *Saint Ignace*, had been retired immediately after the *Chief Wawatam*'s entry into service and her engines given to her smaller namesake. Thus the second *Sainte Marie*, more than amply powered for her size and equipped with a bow propeller, was an

ice-breaker par excellence. Back-up boat for the *Chief* throughout her career, she lasted until 1961 largely as a result of winter leases as an ice-breaker to the Lake Carriers Association.

It was the *Chief*'s ice-breaking abilities that saved her too for so many years; on more than one occasion she had been laid up in favor of a tug-barge operation, only to be brought back in the winter months when the barges stalled in the heavy "windrow"—i. e. piled up and compacted—ice of the Straits. For a time the *Chief Wawatam* appeared to have more lives than a cat, and it can only be considered a miracle that she lasted as long as she did.

For instance, an article in the April 18, 1968, issue of the the *St. Ignace Republican* had this lead: "*Chief Wawatam*, for 57 years the largest ice-breaking railway ferry in the world, is dead." So she was, for a time at least, as tug *Muskegon* and barge *Manistee* (the cut-down hull, ironically, of *Ann Arbor No. 3*) took over the cross-Straits service, which they operated until the following January, when ice brought the

The *Chief* introduced a new and more handsome profile to the Straits in 1911.—ALL, STEVE ELVE COLLECTION

71520 CAR FERRY, CHIEF WAWATAM, BATTLING WITH THE ICE, STRAITS OF MACKINAW

Chief Wawatam back to life once more.

A similar scenario, with all the same players, had occured back in 1965, while the *Chief* was drydocked for six months at Manitowoc for major repairs, particularly the rebuilding of her boilers. In the course of the early 1960's they had deteriorated to the point where operation with the normal steam pressure of 185 pounds per inch had become unsafe. For a month in the early summer of 1964, the *Chief* had endured perhaps the ultimate indignity: being pushed back and forth across the Straits by tug *John Purves*, while emergency boiler work was accomplished. Just enough steam was kept up to

activate such auxiliary functions as the steam steerer and the winch to raise the sea gate.

It was the opening of the Mackinac Bridge on November 1, 1957, that had definitively signaled the end of the *Chief's* untroubled youth. After that, the mail moved to trucks, and the proud designation "U. S. Mail," for years carried prominently above the vessel's name on the bow, became obsolete. By 1960, the number of loaded freight cars transported had dropped to 15,877, from 34,786 in 1951—a decline of well over 50 percent in less than a decade. In 1961 the *Sainte Marie* was sold, and the Mackinac Transportation Company became a one-boat operation for the first time since 1893. By 1964 loaded cars dropped to 7,169, and Mackinac Transportation petitioned the ICC for permission to discontinue its Straits service—a request that would be repeatedly rebuffed.

Mackinac Transportation had been formed in 1881 to operate break-bulk steamers across the Straits. The company was a joint subsidiary of three railroads: the Detroit, Mackinac & Marquette Railway, which in 1886 became the Duluth, South Shore & Atlantic; the Grand Rapids & Indiana, later absorbed by the Pennsylvania Railroad; and the Michigan Central, which became part of the New York Central. Mackinac Transportation perked along through the decades essentially unchanged until Penn Central came into being in 1968, reducing the number of partners to two. Then, after Conrail's formation in 1976 resulted in the demise of the PC-controlled boat line, the State of Michigan stepped in—as it also did with Ann Arbor and, briefly at least, Chessie as well—and the *Chief* was conveyed to the Straits Corporation.

Since the *Chief* provided the all-important northern connection for the State's new Michigan Northern Railway, formed to operate ex-PC trackage not taken by Conrail, a Michigan Northern subsidiary—the Boat Company—eventually took over the service on December 1, 1982. Earlier, Michigan had ordered Soo Line, still one-third owner of the *Chief*, to operate the Straits service. After four months of this, Soo refused to continue, so Michigan then had contracted with the Detroit & Mackinac Railway to operate the boat, securing her future for a time. Through the summer of 1979 the venerable *Chief* once more averaged two round trips a day, five days a week—a dramatic increase from the one trip a week that had been the nadir, reached in the years immediately preceding. More apparent good news came in July 1979, when the Michigan Transportation Commission rejected plans to replace the *Chief* with an integrated tug-barge operation, while also authorizing a consultant to study her possible conversion to oil firing and to estimate the cost of repairs needed to reverse the years of deferred maintenance under Penn Central.

Such conversion never came to pass, though the *Chief* was drydocked at Bay Shipbuilder's at Sturgeon Bay, Wisconsin, in October 1983, for repairs of tank-top welds, some rivet-tightening, repainting of the hull below the water line, and recertification by the Coast Guard. But time was running out for the *Chief*, and her last crossing of the waters where she'd spent her entire career came in August 1984, when the Soo Line slip at St. Ignace was found to need repairs. In 1986, Soo was given permission to abandon its St. Ignace-Trout Lake line, the only Upper Peninsula rail link to the ferry, thus unequivocally eliminating the *Chief*'s function.

For four years she sat at her Mackinaw City mooring, costing some $112,000 annually just for maintenance, docking, security and

insurance. Meanwhile, recognizing that the vessel was an invaluable and irreplacable piece of maritime history, preservationists mounted an energetic, vocal, and ultimately futile campaign for her retention as a museum ship or restaurant. Unswayed by sentiment and history, the Michigan Transportation Commission in October 1988 voted to sell the *Chief* for $110,000—substantially more than any of the preservation bidders offered—to Purvis Marine Limited, a Canadian towing firm. Thus it came to pass that Frank Kirby's proud car ferry was towed to Sault Ste. Marie, Ontario, where she was ignominiously pared down into a barge, and her

The *Chief* steams off across the mist-shrouded Straits.—KARL ZIMMERMANN

Nearing the end of a long career, the *Chief* approaches the slip at Mackinaw City, where a weathered warning sign gives ghostly testimony to New York Central heritage.—BOTH PHOTOS, ROGER COOK

superstructure and upper hull scrapped.

Though this hull still floats—and, mockingly, still wears the name *"Chief Wawatam"*—the real vessel of that name is history. Only in memory will she announce her departure from St. Ignace or Mackinaw City with a single, startling blast of her deep-throated steam whistle. Only in the mind's eye can you watch as she backs silently and majestically out into the Straits of Mackinac and, once clear of the slip, begins to turn almost imperceptibly to face the opposite shore. Slowly,

like Monstro the Whale closing its mouth, the bow sea gate lowers, and the *Chief* begins her one-hour crossing. Minutes pass, and the sky is smudged with coal smoke, hung against the clouds by a trio of firemen sweating below the waterline. Your attention wanders, distracted perhaps by some frolicsome gulls. More minutes pass, and the *Chief Wawatam* grows small until, suddenly, you look up once more and she has vanished into the mists of time hanging over the Straits of Mackinac.

Once loaded, the *Chief* backs out to begin her familiar voyage to St. Ignace.—Roger Cook

ACKNOWLEDGEMENTS

Any research on Lake Michigan car ferries inevitably begins with George W. Hilton's THE GREAT LAKES CAR FERRIES, the standard work on the subject. My copy, ever at my elbow during this project, is well-thumbed. Other books and articles consulted are listed below in the bibliography.

Essential information and material came from many quarters. Steve Elve provided a wealth of photographs and memorabilia from his extensive collection. Thomas W. Dixon Jr., president of the Chesapeake & Ohio Historical Society, opened that group's vast resources of photographs and brochures, giving generously of his own time in the process. William F. Howes Jr. shared research and materials, and John S. Ingles opened his photo collection. Isacco A. Valli, curator and assistant director of the Manitowoc Maritime Museum, Ann C. House, librarian for the Steamship Historical Society of America, and Thomas A. Hawley, director of public relations for Lake Michigan Carferry Service, all assisted as well.

Talented photographers who provided a wide variety of striking images include Tom Post, Mike Schafer, Joe McMillan, Hoang Chi and Roger Cook, Robert E. Mohowski, Russ Porter, and Art Chavez.

My sincerest thanks to all.—K.Z.

BIBLIOGRAPHY

Burgtorf, Frances D. CHIEF WAWATAM: THE STORY OF A HAND-BOMBER. Cheboygan, Mich.: 1976.

Chavez, Art. "3.5 MILLION MILES AND STILL SAILING: A TRIBUTE TO LAKE MICHIGAN'S TRAIN AND AUTO FERRY CITY OF MIDLAND 41," SEA CLASSICS, XXII (September 1989), 48-55; (October 1989), 46-51.

Elve, Steven Dale. "THE MILWAUKEE REMEMBERED," TELESCOPE (GREAT LAKES MARITIME INSTITUTE), XXIX (March/April 1980), 41-43.

Fey, Lewis. "LAKE MICHIGAN'S FLOATING RAILROADS," TRAINS, IX (August 1949), 46-49.

Frederickson, Arthur C. and Lucy F. PICTORIAL HISTORY OF THE C&O TRAIN AND AUTO FERRIES AND PERE MARQUETTE LINE STEAMERS. Frankfort, Mich.: Revised edition, 1965.

Hilton, George W. "GREAT LAKES CAR FERRIES: AN ENDANGERED SPECIES," TRAINS, XXXV (January 1975), 42-51.

Hilton, George W. THE GREAT LAKES CAR FERRIES. Berkley: Howell-North Books, 1962.

Horowitz, Steve. "THE LAST VOYAGE OF THE S.S. BADGER," ANCHOR NEWS (MANITOWOC MARITIME MUSEUM), XI (March/April 1980), 22-28.

Howes, William F. Jr. "C&O RAILWAY'S LAKE MICHIGAN CARFERRIES." Paper delivered to The Lexington Group in Transportation History, Milwaukee, Wis. September 25, 1992.

Wiening, Paul G. "THOSE CLASSY CLASSIC CARFERRIES," TELESCOPE (GREAT LAKES MARITIME INSTITUTE), XXX (January/February 1981), 3-9.